ELIANA

ELIANA
GOD HAS ANSWERED

CANDACE MARIE CHARBONNÉ

XULON ELITE

Xulon Press Elite
2301 Lucien Way #415
Maitland, FL 32751
407.339.4217
www.xulonpress.com

Professional photography by Kristen Nicotra of KArtocin Photography:

Note from author:

The events and conversations in this book have been set down to the best of the author's ability, although some names and details have been changed to protect the privacy of individuals.

Scripture quotations taken from the Holy Bible, New International Version (NIV). Copyright © 1973, 1978, 1984, 2011 by Biblica, Inc.™. Used by permission. All rights reserved.

Paperback ISBN-13: 978-1-66287-617-2
Ebook ISBN-13: 978-1-66287-618-9

Dedication

When I started to share my heart and journey after Eliana died, I had many inclinations there was a story being written by God and my purpose was to share it for His Glory. Several family members and friends unknowingly confirmed this over the past two years with my answer always being the same: it was not the right time.

Like any faithful servant, I was waiting to be told when that right time was, and prayed for God's guidance in this regard. On New Year's Day 2023, my answer came with great clarity. That day, God put on my heart that 2023 was the year I would write and publish Eliana's story. As I started the process almost immediately, I decided I wanted to finish it by her second birthday on February 18, 2023. On February 17, 2023, exactly two years after her heart stopped beating, I submitted the final manuscript to the publisher for editing and pre-production as a birthday present to our sweet girl in Heaven.

To my beautiful daughter, Eliana Elizabeth Charbonné: Being your mother and a witness to your life and God-given purpose has been one of the greatest honors of my life. Your life has given my life newfound purpose and deepened that purpose beyond imagination, and I am grateful for the strengthening of my faith gained through my love for you. We are forever connected as only the spirits of a mother and a child can be; you are a part of me, and I am a part of you and no time nor distance will ever change that. I look forward to our eternity together in paradise.

To my husband, Ross: Thank you for being my protector when I needed you to be; for holding things together when they were falling apart; for being the voice of reason when things didn't make sense; for your faith; and for your unconditional love. God knew I could not do this life without you.

To Alexander, Natalie, and Jeremiah: I love you more than my own life and then some. Each of you are a gift to me from God. You inspire me daily and help me to learn and grow as a person by merely being your mother. I pray you always walk in Faith, grow closer to Christ always and share your bright lights with the world for God's Glory.

To my parents, grandmother, and faithful family members: Thank you for the foundation of faith you provided me in my formative years and for all your prayers and support.

To my family, pastors, friends and colleagues who supported us through it all. We are so grateful for you and your love and support. Thank you will never suffice.

To Aunty Kay thank you for all your time and effort proofreading the book.

Above all, this book is dedicated to my Lord and Savior Jesus Christ without whom I would not have survived the greatest tragedy of my life and to whom I give eternal thanks for every blessing in my life. Specifically, I thank God the Father, God the Son and God the Holy Spirit for the love, strength, comfort, courage, guidance and strengthening of faith over the past two years and I pray that every word in this book glorifies His Holy Name and fulfills every purpose set forth by the Lord my God.

Psalm 86:12: *I will give thanks to You, O Lord my God, with all my heart, And will glorify Your name forever.*

Chapter 1

Late on Tuesday, February 16, 2021, my husband Ross and I sat on the couch talking for a couple hours after he got home from work at around 9:30-10 PM. We sat and talked about our respective workdays which were long and jam-packed and what our Wednesday looked like, which was also jam-packed. We talked about the kids and how life was about to change with Eliana set to arrive any day. We talked about how we really needed to finish the nursery over the weekend and laughed because we were so behind on getting things organized this time. But in the grand scheme of things, this was our 3rd baby, so we were confident that we had all the essentials already in place. Owning over nine car seats spread across several countries, we were confident that if push came to shove, we could install an infant car seat quickly with no issue. Eliana was moving as usual and enjoying my very reclined position on the couch. I was telling Ross she was moving quite a bit earlier and the kids were, as usual, poking her, playing with her and talking to her. Ross put his hand on my belly and started to do the same. She actually made a huge turn and my whole belly moved from right to left. Ross was like, "Whoa, that's big" to which I said, "yep, she does that often because she has quite a bit of space in there due to my excess amniotic fluid."

We finally went to bed at around 12 AM with me only waking once at 4 AM to use the bathroom. For the entirety of my pregnancy, I had always said how good Eliana was to sleep when I slept, so it wasn't unusual I didn't notice anything at 4 AM.

As I did on every school/workday, I woke up at 7 AM to get the kids up and ready for school and myself ready for work. When I woke up, I did make note that Eliana was a bit quiet but thought that she just needed some breakfast to get going. That morning was the same as practically every morning. Rush, rush, rush to get the kids ready for school, make lunch boxes and get out the door to barely make it to school on time. I actually recall telling the kids we needed to do better to be early because once Eliana arrived, it would be a lot more complicated getting ready and to school on time.

With no time to make myself breakfast before leaving, I was hungry and in need of food. Craving avocado toast from the Pie Lady in town, I decided to stop there to grab breakfast after school drop off and before heading back home for my second to last day of work before my maternity leave started on Friday.

In true hungry pregnant lady fashion, I inhaled the food in the car and then started to drive right away. At the time, I assumed the reason I couldn't feel Eliana moving was because I was driving; small movements are hard to feel while the car is in motion.

I got home, checked some emails and had a 30-minute meeting with my intern. In the haste of the workday already off to the races, I decided to pause and focus on Eliana just to check in on her as she was not active enough to be noticeable, but I was also very distracted with work. I decided to get some apple juice and lay down for a minute to focus. Soon after drinking apple juice, Eliana would usually be doing backflips; however, I didn't notice much movement. So at this point, I was concerned enough to call the doctor.

The doctor's office indicated they couldn't see me in the office until the afternoon but didn't want me to wait that long, so they asked me to go to OB triage in the hospital where I was supposed to deliver for a Non-Stress Test (NST) to check on the baby.

Due to the excess amniotic fluid and my maternal age, I was having NSTs every week since 32 weeks, so it was not uncommon for me and this pregnancy. I actually had my weekly NST scheduled for the next day.

I hopped in the car and took my hospital bag just in case, as my mind thought, the worst case scenario would be that I would be rushed in to emergency surgery, should Eliana be in distress.

Our last full scan for Eliana was at 35 weeks 6 days (two weeks before) where she measured in the 80th percentile and, with the exception of her dilated kidney issue which was stable, she was fine. Dilated kidneys in babies in utero are fairly common and once stable, it isn't cause for great concern. Additionally, our daughter Natalie had the same condition in utero and after birth it cleared up on its own within six months. As it was fairly common and we had been through it before with Natalie, we weren't overly concerned as it was stable, no better and no worse. All professional advice indicated the best place for her was in my belly.

I knew Ross had a busy morning with back-to-back calls until the afternoon, so I sent him a text just to let him know I was a bit concerned about Eliana's movement this morning and was headed to OB triage at the hospital to check it out. With COVID policies in place, your spouse wasn't allowed at appointments with you, so I was used to going on my own and didn't see the need to pull Ross out of meetings to go with me because it was just another NST and I was probably overreacting.

When I got to the hospital, I thought to myself, "The last parking spot I just got was pretty far from the front door, so I should be proactive and take my suitcase with me to avoid the long walk back to the car in case they need to admit me."

I checked in and waited for the nurse to start the NST. She moved the Doppler all over my stomach to see if she could find Eliana's heartbeat. The fact she couldn't find it was not a cause for alarm as it had happened a couple times before in pervious NSTs and we always found it. I mentioned to the nurse that a couple of weeks ago, when we had problems finding her heartbeat, the nurse put me on my side and we found it. We tried that and at one point, we both thought we heard a faint something, so I continued to not worry. The nurse then said, "I'm going to get the ultrasound machine." When she returned, she came in with the ultrasound machine and the doctor on call from the practice where I had been going.

The doctor introduced herself because I didn't know her. The practice was huge with nine practitioners, and I only managed to meet half of them. She indicated she was going to do an ultrasound to see what was going on. At the time, I didn't put two and two together that they were quite concerned which was indicative by where the doctor was standing and how she was purposefully blocking the screen from my view. Still, at this point, I was concerned but not worried. She asked the nurse where the color button was on the ultrasound machine, but the nurse didn't know so they called another nurse in the room who showed her where the button was. After they switched on the color button, the doctor turned to me and said, "Candace, I am so sorry; there is no heartbeat. The baby is gone."

I said in absolute and total disbelief, "WHAT! What do you mean she has no heartbeat?"

She then proceeded to show me on the screen, "This is her heart; it should be flickering but there is no flicker. There also should be color, indicating blood is pumping and there is no blood flow." With tears in her eyes, my eyes, the nurses' eyes, she said "She's gone. I'm so sorry."

Even though I could see what she was saying, I was still in shock and disbelief that this was what she was saying. I said, "You need to get someone else to check. Get another doctor to check."

The other doctor came quickly and checked and said, "I agree with the other doctor. The baby has no heartbeat and is gone."

The doctor who initially delivered the bad news then said, "Is there someone you need to call? We need to admit you and figure out the next steps for delivery."

I tried desperately to get a hold of Ross who was still in meetings. I called him several times consecutively with no answer, just voicemail. Eventually, he texted me and said, "What's up?" I responded, they are saying the baby has no heartbeat and is gone." Within a minute of sending that text, Ross called me.

He said, "What do you mean she has no heartbeat? What does that even mean?" I said, Babe, they are saying the baby is dead; she is gone."

He said, "But I don't understand. I was feeling her moving fine last night. How could she be gone?"

I said, "I don't know, but they showed me the screen and that's what it's saying. I also don't understand either."

I kept thinking to myself, how is this even possible? I'm 37 weeks 5 days. She was fine."

When Ross arrived, they said, "we are admitting you and taking you upstairs to Labor and Delivery where we will talk about the next steps."

And so, my biggest test of Faith began at 12 AM on Ash Wednesday, February 17, 2021.

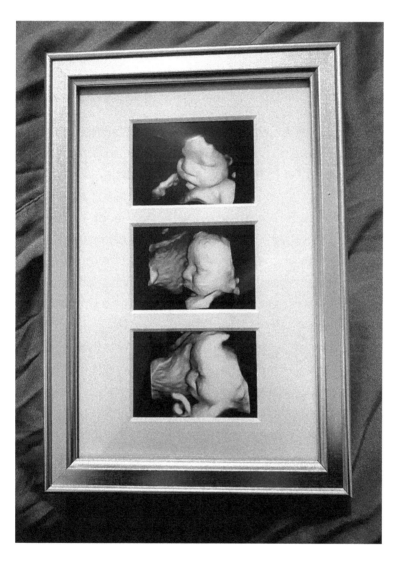

Eliana at 35 weeks 6 days via ultrasound

Chapter 2

As they rolled me upstairs in the wheelchair, I swore I felt Eliana move. I thought maybe, just maybe they were wrong. Or that by some great miracle, she was alive. When we got to the room, I asked the doctor if they could do another ultrasound and check. At this point, this was the 4th ultrasound to check, and the 1st one Ross was seeing. They showed Ross the same thing they showed me three times before. "Here's her heart; there is no flicker and no color. We are sorry." Again, we let those words and that reality sink in.

The doctor came in and introduced another doctor as they were switching shifts. Again, this was another doctor I had not met because the practice was so big. In a way, it was probably better to be with a doctor I wasn't familiar with as I had so many questions for the ones I did know.

The nurses also introduced themselves. Everyone was sorry and everyone was crying.

Here we were; our baby we had been looking forward to since the day we found out we were pregnant 8.5 months ago (and even before that) was dead and now the doctors want us (really me) to make a decision on how I wanted to proceed to deliver her. Definitely not the delivery conversation we ever expecting to have or were prepared for. My first response was, "Take me upstairs to do a C-Section. I want her out now so I can hold her; maybe there is something you can still do to save her."

The doctor assured me that even if they took me to do a C-Section, the outcome wouldn't change. He said that my recovery while grieving will be longer with a C-Section and that for six weeks, I would have a constant physical reminder of what happened which will be, in the long run, harder for my emotional healing. In hindsight, this was true.

She then said they could do an aggressive induction which would hopefully go fast, once my body remembers what it's like to be in labor or we can do a regular induction and see how long it takes. I weighed all options and said, "Give me the most aggressive option and as much pain medication as possible." I didn't see the need to be laboring and in pain on top of the emotional pain I was feeling so deeply.

Ross was in agreement with the plan and told the doctor, "I don't care what you do as long as you keep my wife alive. I can only handle one death today."

The anesthesiologist came in to administer the epidural. This required me to hold on to the nurse and not move. I had to control my breathing. As the young nurse and I synced our breathing as we were about to start the next leg of this painful birthing journey, I could tell she was crying. After the epi was in and I had a moment with the nurse, I asked her if she had ever been present for a situation like ours. She said no; it was her first time and that she would remember us forever and pray for us. I felt so bad for her. I think I even apologized for putting her through this situation. She was so kind in saying, "I'm so sorry this happened to you and your husband and that you had to go through this." The more senior nurse of the two said she had been a nurse for over twenty years and whether it's your first time or 20th or 100th time, it's never easy. It's just so heartbreaking for them to witness the pain of the parents and unfortunately, it happens more than people think. Their empathy and compassion for us was really moving and helped us through such an impossible situation.

Labor was long. Though I wasn't in physical pain, the emotional pain and the dread of what came next was not good.

Ten hours after being induced, it was finally time to push. They asked me, just like with Alexander and Natalie, what I would like to do once she came out and I said the exact same for Eliana; I wanted to hold her right away.

I wasn't sure if it was the situation or COVID, but there was only one nurse and one doctor in the room for delivery. This resulted in Ross having to assist with supporting my right leg as I pushed. I could tell he was in pain, not a physical pain but an emotional pain that causes you to be sick to your stomach and in physical pain as a result. His face said it all. I tried to tell him to keep looking at me but it was impossible. I think these are some of the images that kept him up at night and still haunt him today.

After thirty minutes or so of pushing, Eliana Elizabeth Charbonné was stillborn at 1:58 AM on February 18, 2021.

As I had requested, they put her in a blanket and gave her to me right away. I just stared at her deep red face, dark red lips and sealed shut eyes that would never open. We were all very aware that the room was absent of the cries of a newborn fresh out the womb. The silence was deafening and continued to be for months after.

With the exception of being dead and all that came with that in terms of her appearance, she was perfect. Absolutely beautiful. Ross and I said to her, "You just topped Alexander for best looking baby fresh out the womb and, well, our beautiful Natalie as a fresh newborn wasn't ever in the running." She actually reminded us so much of Alexander and could have been his little clone, had it not been for her full head of black hair! All the nurses that came in kept saying how beautiful she was; we didn't know if they were just being kind, but we really couldn't stop staring at her beautiful little face and thinking of what she would have grown up to look like amongst so many other wonderful qualities.

We were heartbroken. As I held her lifeless body, I kept thinking to myself how was this our reality? She was no smaller than we remembered Alexander and Natalie being. She was a whole, fully formed 7lbs 1oz ready to take home baby. How was this reality? I couldn't stop thinking that babies born younger than Eliana go in to the NICU and make it. She was our almost 38-week-old baby; how is this even possible? Reconciling reality at that point and for so many months after was tremendously hard.

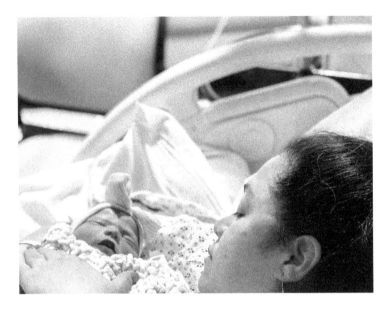

At this point, the nurses offered us two options: they could take Eliana and give us some time alone and even never bring her back if we wish or we could keep her as long as we wanted and they would bring something they call a coddle cot so we could keep her cold in order to slow the decomposition of her body.

Once the coddle cot arrived, Ross kept saying, "Instead of one of those beds that keep the baby warm like French fries, we have a bed to put her on ice. So unnatural."

Truth be told, the whole situation felt unnatural. With Alexander and Natalie at this point after delivery, they had already latched, nursing for the first time and in Natalie's case, three to four times. They had both gone to the nursery and come back all fresh and clean with that intoxicating new baby smell. They had cried their little lungs out, opened their eyes, melted our hearts and got loads of kisses and snuggles. With Eliana, it was just quiet and cold with the absence of everything normal or natural. The only thing familiar was our love for her which was the same we felt for her siblings, but this love came with heartache; this love hurt.

I encouraged Ross to hold her but he didn't want to. Eventually, with much hesitation, he did. As he took her from me to hold her for the first time, the pain on his face was just heartbreaking. That look of "You were fine and now you are gone." The look of how is this even possible. That helpless parent look that says, "I was supposed to protect you and I couldn't; we couldn't." A pain you can only feel holding your dead child's lifeless body in your arms.

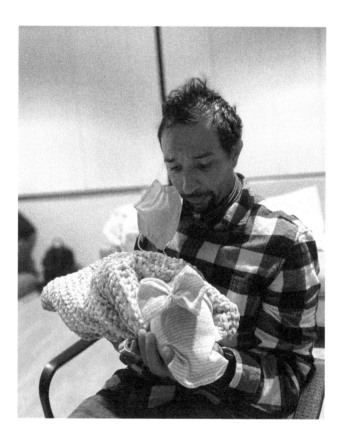

At around 4 AM, I noticed that I kept smelling something strange on my person and thought maybe I just need a shower. My nose has always been quite sensitive to smell, but I wasn't sure what I was smelling. At that point, the nurses said they could take Eliana to do a foot mold keepsake and footprints while I had a shower. I said okay and went to have a shower, finally able to walk after the epidural wore off.

After my shower, I was now very sure the smell would be gone. They brought her back for me right away as I wanted but the smell wasn't gone. I then realized that not only was the new baby smell not there but there was a smell of death and it was coming from my baby. This was very hard to reconcile. I eventually forced myself to get used to the smell because the only other option was to put her down and I could literally feel my minutes with her counting down so that wasn't an option.

They then moved us downstairs to recovery to start the next part of our journey.

Chapter 3

We got downstairs at around 4:30 AM and were just exhausted; emotionally, physically and mentally exhausted.

As we got settled in the new room, our nurse from upstairs introduced us to a new set of nurses. This floor was quiet and only thinking back on it now, I realize I didn't recall hearing one baby cry so we must have been in another section of the maternal ward that was only for people in our situation.

I waited for them to bring Eliana back to us as they had to be the ones to bring her down. Once she arrived, I got situated on the new bed, had my vitals taken yet again and then asked to be handed Eliana. Back together again. Even though she was dead, her little body gave me such comfort. After all, it was only a few hours ago she was in my belly.

Ross, who was looking like he was ready to pass out from exhaustion, tried to convince me to get some sleep by saying "We" should get some sleep; it's going to be a long day. I couldn't argue with that. It was probably going to be a long day. I got him to help me prop a pillow under the arm I was dominantly holding Eliana with, as my arm started to get tired. I agreed to try to get some sleep so he would go sleep without feeling bad. Truth be told, I really didn't want to sleep. I just wanted to stare at her as I knew our time was limited. Eventually, I laid her on the bed next to me and slept for 45 mins just snuggling her. I even joked with her that I had done this with Natalie in the hospital and a nurse yelled at me for co-sleeping, but I didn't think in her case any nurses would be yelling at me.

The sun started to come up and we could see the snow coming down. Yep, it was another snowstorm / ice storm. The kids were home from school due to snow, not COVID, as they luckily had to be back in school five days a week since the previous September.

With the sun finally up, I could get started on taking some pictures of Eliana in the natural light. I wanted to remember her little face forever and taking pictures and videos was the best way I knew how to do that.

I woke poor Ross up to tell him go shower and get off the couch as I needed the couch and the window to take pics. I said to him, "Eliana's pictures are going on the family wall at home just like everyone else so I need to do a newborn photo session for her right now." Though the hospital had indicated they would take pictures of her as part of our keepsakes, I really wanted to do this for her and for us and the kids. I had, after all, done Natalie's newborn pictures and knew I was quite particular in what I liked and couldn't chance this task to anyone else as this was my only opportunity.

Honestly, in hindsight, it was a good thing I took 211 pictures and four videos that day as when we finally got home and looked at the pictures the sweet nurses took in the hospital, Ross and I were horrified and said we never wanted to see the pictures again. She just looked so dead! What a terrible reminder of what happened!

As I positioned and posed her little lifeless body all over, I apologized to her for moving her so much. Talking to her,

I said, "Well, girl, luckily Mummy in her past life considered quitting her day job to do newborn and family photography. So don't worry; I'll fix up your photos and it will be worth the effort."

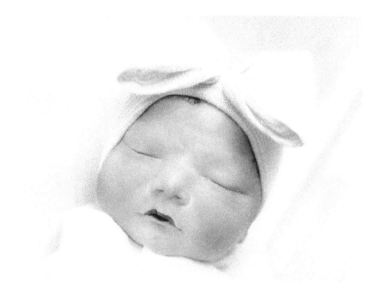

I swapped out the big fluffy blanket for a nice pink muslin and swaddled her as there was a huge battle wound from the birthing on the left side of her neck that I wanted to hide for the pics. I asked Ross to dig in my suitcase to see what else I had in there that we could use and out came the sign with her name. I had bought the sign over a month ago and planned to use it to announce her birth in the hospital. But seeing the beautiful sign and the fact it wouldn't be used for the purpose I intended pained me and I just didn't see the point in using it. Ross kept bringing the sign and said, "No, take a few with it. Yes, it's not being used for what you intended and this isn't how we expected it to go, but it looks nice and, dead or not, that's her name." He was right so I forced myself to use it and really was so happy I did in the end.

The pictures were so important to me. At home, we have a large wall with just pictures of our little family. It is essentially a photo journey of our life in chronological order and I wanted Eliana to be as present on the wall as Natalie and Alexander are to represent her place in our family, even if she was only with us physically a brief time.

After Ross took a few pictures of me with Eliana during her newborn shoot, I encouraged him to hold her again so

I could take some pictures of them together. The pain on his face as he held her was still there and continued to be there for months later as he looked at her pictures or saw the space where her ashes rest in our home. Even to present times Ross still gets very emotional looking at any unedited pictures of Eliana as it's just too painful. On the other hand, I can look at any version as the pain is the same either way.

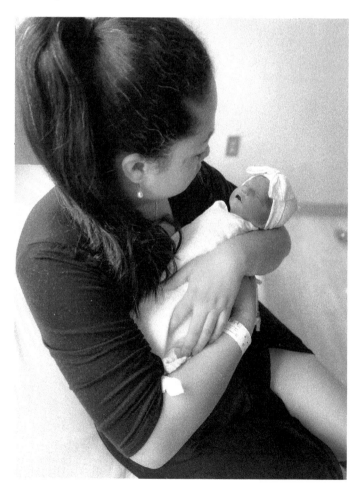

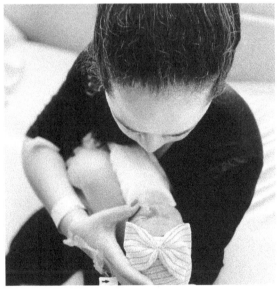

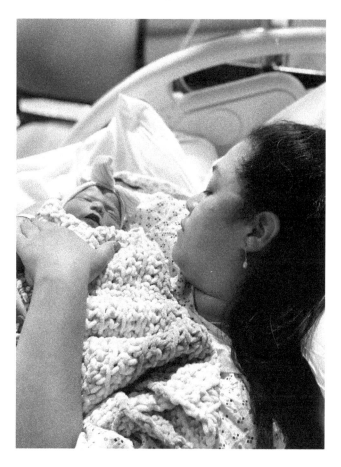

I recall at one point later that day I even had us take a few selfies with her for good measure because, just like Alexander and Natalie, I thought Eliana should also have selfies with us and we would never have the opportunity again. As I reviewed our sorry attempts at selfies with our sweet Eliana, I said to Ross, "we can do better for her sake. She shouldn't have every picture with us looking sad and sour, we should smile at least for one; after all, we love her and she deserves us to smile." And so, we smiled as best we could, even though it hurt.

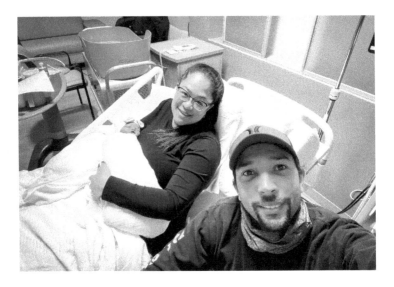

At some point, just after our newborn shoot, the third doctor on call came in. I had met this doctor before in the office. As she greeted us, she was also crying and also sorry. After the formalities, as I call it, she checked me and indicated that everything looked good physically and that they could release me that morning, if I wanted. She assured me there was no rush and I could stay as long as I thought I needed which could be days. It was entirely up to me.

This brought up so much emotion and anxiety. The time to leave Eliana was near and in reality, it was up to me. I was so torn. As badly as I wanted to go home to Alexander and Natalie, I couldn't bear the thought of leaving Eliana. Yet, another unnatural occurrence. Had everything gone as planned, I wouldn't have to choose between my children; we would just all be together.

I also started to worry that Alexander would start to figure out the reason that we were gone was to have the baby. We talked to him and Natalie about what would happen and that I could be gone for a few days but then would come home with their sister. I started to worry that if he started to piece things together, he would start to ask questions. In the absence of his questions being answered, would they start anticipating and assume their sister they had waited so long for was coming home with Mummy and Daddy soon, just like we spoke about?

What were we going to tell them?

How were we going to break their hearts?

They were totally attached and bonded with her. They talked to her every day since I told them she could hear them around twenty weeks. They poked her and felt her move daily. They must have told her their names and who they were to her dozens of times. They sang to her, told her what they would do with her when she came out and most importantly, how much they loved her and were so excited and couldn't wait to meet her.

What were we going to say that would break their hearts?

How would they take the news?

And how would we navigate the grief?

These questions and overall worry about my other babies started to give me anxiety and cause additional pain in such a complex way.

Now, I was struggling between wanting to stay and spend every minute with Eliana that I could and wanting to go home to Alexander and Natalie to hug them and spare them any further false excitement and anticipation. The thought of their oncoming pain and disappointment made me feel sick. I just needed to hug them, but I knew that would mean leaving Eliana behind.

How could I choose between staying with Eliana and going home to Alexander and Natalie?

How could I choose between my children?

Chapter 4

Y EARS AGO, THROUGH different trials and journeys, I
began the practice of letting things go and letting God
take control by saying, "Lord, Your will be done." It has
honestly taken me years and years of practice to get to the
point where I can truly let something go and say, "Lord, Your
will be done" within minutes of something going wrong
which, I acknowledge, is not easy.

At first, when I started to practice this, it would be
months of agonizing over what was troubling me before I
could let things or worries or my personal plans go before I
said with my whole heart, "Lord, Your will be done."

Over the years, the time it took to release things reduced.
Months turned into weeks, which then turned into days,
which then turned into hours and now minutes. As I said
before, it was very hard in the beginning, but I eventually
realized if I swam against the current or direction of God's
plan, then things were so much harder and out of control.
However, if I swam with the current, though in some cases
the waters were still rough, challenging and hard, I was
tooled and guided by God to manage through.

In some cases, I was eventually granted enlightenment
at the end of some journeys or at pit stops to see the purpose of each journey and get a small glimpse at the "why"
it was meant to be.

I believe now all this practice was part of my preparation for this moment and this journey.

When I initially walked into OB triage at the hospital and was being checked in, I recall making eye contact with one of the nurses. We never spoke, but I noticed our connection when our eyes met.

Before Ross arrived and after they told me Eliana's heart stopped, that same nurse "randomly" came in and said to me in her thick Caribbean accent as my eyes now filled with tears, "This is part of God's plan. I am praying for you." This reminder was necessary in that moment and only now looking back on it, I know she was sent by God to remind me as things started to fall apart.

While in OB triage, after I called Ross and made arrangements for the kids to be picked up from school, I called my mom to let my parents and family know what was going on. I recall, at one point in the conversation with my mom, she said, "I am praying for a miracle. They can check again and find out they were wrong. She will be ok." I remember responding to her, "Mom, they have checked twice and she is gone. Yes, I believe that God who parted the Red Sea for Moses and brought Lazarus back to life can bring Eliana back to life, but if it's not HIS will, then HIS will be done."

Over the years since starting to pray the Rosary regularly, I would only and still only ever pray one prayer for myself. I pray to be guided by the Holy Spirit to see my path and the strength to walk it. This prayer was never more needed than for this situation.

Since we had been upstairs in labor and delivery, basically waiting through the 10 hours of labor, Ross and I started to talk about how we wanted to navigate the situation regarding our feelings over Eliana's death and this painful journey that just started. It was clear that in order for us to survive this together, we needed to be on the same page regarding the way forward.

There was a clear fork in the road for us, faith wise.

God giving mankind free will gave us a choice.

As I saw it, we had two choices. We could be justifiably angry our baby girl died. Angry at God for allowing this to happen which would totally shatter our faith or we could accept that for whatever reason, it was part of God's plan.

Ross then said, "Well, being angry will not bring her back, so I don't see the point in being angry."

I agreed and said, "Yes, anger is toxic. It's like a poison and that's not an emotion I have space for in this situation; it will just make it harder."

I also said, "If I truly believe Eliana is, indeed, in Heaven and there is eternal life after this life which I do and I go down the path of being angry with God, do I believe I will be where she is in Heaven when I die? Am I willing to chance that outcome? No, when my turn comes, I want there to be no pit stops on my way to Heaven and it's a "beam me up Scottie" type of situation with the gates wide open so I can see my child and my Friend right away."

Throughout that night, I kept saying to Ross, "Blessed are those who suffer, for theirs is the kingdom of Heaven." After saying this a few times, I joked with Ross saying, "Well, based on this tragic turn of events, one of us just got a one-way ticket to Heaven and seeing that I am pretty confident they will let me in, this must be your ticket!"

He laughed and said, "Probably."

After this, but at some point before Eliana was born, our labor and delivery nurse was talking to us with tears in her eyes saying that it just pained her to see this happen to beautiful couples like us. I took her hand and squeezed it as the tears hit her mask and said, "Don't cry… just pray for us; we will be ok because God is with us. If this is His will, then He will give us the strength and means to get through it as He never gives you more than you can handle."

She then said, "Here I'm supposed to be comforting you and here you are comforting me."

And so, on Ash Wednesday 2021, Ross and I decided together to accept our beloved Eliana's death was our cross to carry in this life; this would be our painful path to walk but that we would not walk it alone; we would walk it with Jesus.

As with most things, this is always easier said than done.

Chapter 5

Sometime after the photoshoot, as I settled back into the bed with Eliana, the negative thoughts and doubts started to creep into my mind [enters the devil].

Was this my fault?

I recalled holding Eliana and feeling a weird crick from her neck as I tried to situate her on my arm. Her neck was so unstable and felt like it was broken. I knew her body was limp, but I also knew what I was feeling.

I started to think to myself, "Oh my God, I broke her neck and killed her. As I literally started to travel down that dark path, the nurse came in to check my vitals again. Ross was in the bathroom and I was alone with the nurse. She could tell I was upset.

So, I decided to ask her if she thought it was possible that I rolled over onto my belly in my sleep and broke Eliana's neck.

As I vocalized the question, I was horrified that the answer could be yes.

The kind nurse said, "This is in no way your fault. We see it happen a lot with stillbirths. Her body was limp because there was no blood flowing in her body. This makes getting a baby who is limp out of the birth canal very difficult."

Though I knew her answer made sense, I couldn't help but think to myself, "She's probably only saying that to make me feel better."

When Ross came out of the bathroom and the nurse left, I told him what I was thinking and what the nurse said. He looked at me with tears in his eyes and said, "No, the nurse is right. It was definitely the doctor; I saw when it happened. The doctor had a very hard time getting her out; this is why she is so banged up. It was like the doctor was trying to pull a rag doll out of a small space except it was our child." I knew in that moment, he wasn't trying to make me feel better; it was just the truth.

This also explained so much of the pain and sickened feeling all over his face while I gave birth to Eliana. It also explained why he couldn't look at unedited pictures of her easily, why it was so hard for him to hold her and why for the first week after we got home, he couldn't sleep.

This was the first of many thoughts like this that threatened my stability on my chosen path to walk in faith.

On top of this, there was also a lot of paperwork and questions which needed to be answered before we left the hospital, questions that you would never be prepared for, especially when discussing your child.

What funeral home would we like to use because someone needs to pick her up when we leave?

Do we want an autopsy done?

Are we going to do a funeral?

Are we going to bury her or cremate her?

Do we want to have the hospital chaplain come to baptize her or pray with us?

There were just so many questions. Some questions, they said, didn't need to be decided until after we left, but we wanted to discuss and figure them out anyway.

The night before, I had called Father Jack, one of our Parish Priests, to ask him to pray for us.

Little did I know he was already aware something was going south since the school pick up that day. He knew I was due any day so when he saw our dear friend Chris picking up the kids, he asked her if it was time. Chris said the look she and Father exchanged in that moment and her words to him, "Father, we need your prayers" was enough for him to know something was going terribly wrong.

Once on the phone with Father Jack, I explained to him that Eliana had died and we weren't sure when she would arrive but wanted to know if he would be able to baptize her before we left the hospital. He said to let him know when she arrived and he will come over to the hospital once they would let him in.

As Eliana arrived at 2 AM, I decided to text Father Jack rather than call and let him know she was out but we would call him in the morning to figure things out.

Early that morning, sometime during the photoshoot, Father Jack called to check in on us and asked if we wanted him to come over.

Looking at the terrible snowstorm outside, Ross and I said to him on the speaker phone that the weather was pretty bad and we didn't want to put him in harm's way and that we would be ok.

Father Jack then said, "I've driven in snowstorms before, so if you need me there, I'm coming. You don't need to worry about me."

Since moving down to South Jersey, we formed a special bond with Father Jack, similar to the relationship my family had with our family priest growing up in Trinidad. Father Jack blessed our home when we moved in, he has blessed every religious pendant, picture, and trinket we had at the time. He blessed our dedicated garden to Our Lady the Blessed

Mother of Jesus and was one of the two priests supporting the school which Alexander and Natalie attended, so we saw him a lot at pick up and the kids saw him during lunch and recess almost every day.

Father Jack insisted that he come and knowing we probably wouldn't be able to stop him at this point, we agreed to ask the nurses if he could come with the related COVID protocols.

We told him we would call him back and buzzed for the nurse. She came in and we asked her if our Priest could come and baptize Eliana.

She said she was not sure but would go ask.

She returned after about 10 minutes and said she checked and he could come with a mask, of course, and to give her his name for the front desk. She then said, "Even if they had said no, the nurses had planned to sneak him in the backdoor for us." This made us laugh.

About an hour after we gave Father Jack the green light to come, he arrived.

He explained to us that Baptism is technically only for the living but that he can do a conditional baptism because we had planned to have her baptized in the church in the future, had the outcome been different.

Just before he started the baptism ceremony, Father Jack explained that in his haste to leave, he put down his holy water bottle when he went for his prayer book and then forgot to pick it back up. So he ended up having to stop at McDonalds to get a cup of water which he could bless, which is why the holy water was in a McDonalds cup!

Ross and I really needed a laugh and that was just funny!

So, with his book of prayers in hand and the McDonald's cup of holy water ready, we started the conditional baptism ceremony for Eliana Elizabeth.

In true Father Jack fashion, his words were uplifting and exactly what we needed to hear in that moment. As we watched her being baptized with the holy water out of the McDonald's cup, we couldn't help but smile.

After the Ceremony and praying with us, we discussed with Father our wish to have a funeral for Eliana. He walked us through the process and also made a recommendation for a funeral home that works well with the church. He assured us the funeral home was very good and that they would make all the arrangements for us.

We also discussed with him cremation vs burial. We explained to him that even though we were pretty certain we would be in NJ a long time, we didn't know if this was where we would be forever. In particular, we were concerned if we ever decided to move back to Trinidad at any point, we would not want to leave Eliana behind in NJ. With cremation, her ashes could be at home with us and if we moved, she could come with us or if I died, she could just go in my coffin and be buried with me. He explained to us all we needed to know regarding this and it helped us to make a final decision.

After Father Jack drank the remainder of the holy water from the McDonald's cup and left, we called the funeral home.

We spoke to the owner whom Father knew personally and discussed with him all the options. Ross did most of the talking, but I had just one question for him.

I asked him, "Once you picked her up tomorrow, would I be able to have access to her while she was at the funeral home?"

He said, "Ma'am, that's usually not our protocol."

I stopped him short and now crying, "Sir, I understand that this is not your protocol, but I need to know if I leave this hospital today and go home and I regretted it, I will be able to see my child again. I need your assurance."

He said, "Ma'am, I understand, we will work something out."

After Eliana was born and everything was done, the doctor asked if we wanted to run extra tests to see if we could determine a cause of death. We agreed to everything: my blood, umbilical cord and placenta related but were uncertain about the autopsy. The doctor had indicated that in most cases, when an autopsy is done, there is a great chance there would be no answer or cause of death found.

This question regarding the autopsy was still pending and we had to answer it before we left, as it required a signature.

Earlier, when I changed Eliana from the big fluffy blanket to the pink swaddle, I noticed she had skin missing from her neck, her left hand and her left ankle. Her little body had been through so much. I wanted to see every scar and every part of her little body but Ross said it was pretty bad and I shouldn't look. So, I swaddled her and never looked.

As we tried to make a final decision on the autopsy, we felt strongly that her little body had already been through so much and that an answer that may never come or that wouldn't bring her back was not worth putting her body through anything more by doing the autopsy. So, we told them no thanks.

In the end, we were so grateful Father Jack came because without him, we wouldn't have had the guidance and help we needed to answer some of these looming and daunting questions. Throughout this time, he has been a real support to us and we are certain he is one of the many people God sent to help us through this impossibly traumatic event.

It was now around 2 PM and one question still remained unanswered. When would we leave?

It was still unanswered and still up to me.

Chapter 6

With the departure of Father Jack, we were alone again. Ross, who was still exhausted, quickly fell asleep on the couch again.

At some point, when Ross was sleeping, I had briefly put Eliana down in the coddle cot to go to the bathroom. When finished in the bathroom, I went straight over to pick her up again. As I picked her up, I noticed her body was getting more and more unstable. I became very aware in that moment that the more I held her, the more her little body was deteriorating. With the constant holding and the picking up and putting down, I was causing more harm to her already fragile little body.

This feeling made me feel selfish. My need for her to be with me was hurting her.

I knew her body needed to be on ice or in a really good freezer and that my not wanting to give her up and go home was dishonoring her body, just like we felt the autopsy would do.

I had reached a turning point.

My instincts as her mother set in and now I needed to protect her from me. I had to let her body go before she deteriorated more. No matter how hard that would be for me, I had to do it for her.

The nurse came in to remove the IV drips and tape I had all over and I said to her, "I would like to be discharged and leave here at 6. Can you make the preparations? How would this work with the baby?"

The nurse gave me several options, including they could come in and take her out the room and I could leave. She also said they could let me leave her in the room with another nurse and then she would take me downstairs.

It was now 4 PM. I had two hours to figure out how I was going to actually do this. How would I say goodbye and leave her?

I continued to hold her, taking videos of how she looked from my vantage point looking down at her perfect little face. I never wanted to forget it and this was the best way I could think of.

Ross eventually woke up. I told him we would be leaving at 6 PM. I think for him, this was a relief, although at no point did I feel he was pressuring me to leave.

I changed my clothes and started to pack up my bags. Thinking ahead, Ross called up room service and insisted I order some food as we would likely have no time to eat once we were home. He was concerned because I hadn't eaten since the avocado toast the day before prior to arriving at the hospital.

I really didn't want anything to eat, but knew he was right. So, I ordered the most appealing thing on the menu at the time, meatloaf and mashed potatoes. It was now 6 PM and we were just getting the food. Reluctantly, I put Eliana down so I could eat. After Ross and I finished our meals, the nurses came back in to have us sign the discharge papers. I was, at this point, back to holding Eliana in the bed. The nurse told Ross he should take the bags down and pull the car upfront and she will bring me down to the front door in the wheelchair.

It was time for Ross to head down as he needed to clear the snow off the car and warm it up after the storm. He touched her forehead with his hand and with tears in his eyes, he said, "Bye, baby, Daddy loves you" and walked out.

That was hard to watch and I was sick thinking my turn was coming momentarily.

I asked the nurses for some time alone with her.

I couldn't stop crying at this point.

I explained to her that we had to go because she needed care we couldn't give her now. I told her the hospital wouldn't let us take her home with us. I said how sorry I was that she couldn't come with us in the car but that Aunty Natalie (my best friend who died in 2011) knew the way to our house and could bring her there. I told her that we had a beautiful unfinished bedroom for her, but she could come sleep in our bedroom, just like Alexander and Natalie did. I told her that our home was her home and she could stay as long as she wanted or just visit; it was up to her.

I kissed her little face all over and told her how much I loved her and wished things could have been different.

I then spoke to Natalie and said, "Friend, you need to take care of my baby girl until I can see you both in Heaven. Take care of her for me. Show her the way to our house. Take care of her."

At this point, the nurses came in and asked me if I wanted them to take her from my arms. I said, "No, I will put her in the cot."

I got off the bed and walked her over to the coddle cot. I kissed and hugged her several more times and then finally gently put her in.

I took a video of her lying there as I stroked her face one last time. I finally bent over to kiss her again and said, "Bye,

Eliana, Mama loves you" and then walked over and sat in the wheelchair.

They placed a purple box of keepsakes on my lap and a bunch of other bags with keepsakes. My lap and arms were full of things but were so empty without Eliana.

The nurse asked me if I was ready and I nodded, not able to speak at this point because of all my tears. The ride down was painful in the most gut-wrenching way and my tears kept flowing silently. I had just given birth to a beautiful baby girl but couldn't leave with her. I had to leave her behind. 37 weeks and 6 days together and we were no longer together.

As we got downstairs, I could see our car out front. The nurse opened the car door and gave me a huge hug. She was also crying. She once again said how sorry she was and would be praying for us. I thanked her, got in and closed the door.

As the door closed, I turned to Ross and totally broke down. My cries in his arms were an uncontrollable cry of pure pain from my shattered heart.

In that moment, Ross said, "There it is," like he was waiting for me to finally break.

These were officially two of the worst days of our lives and it wasn't even over yet.

Now we were headed home to go break the hearts of our other babies. What were we going to say; how could we explain the unexplainable? What were we going to do?

When I was finally able to give Ross his arm back, he started driving. We let Lisa (my aunt) know we were on our way home. Here we go.

After a few deep breaths for us both, we tried to focus on what we were going to say to the kids when we got home.

The only thing we could come up with was that we wanted to tell them together and that we wanted to tell them as much truth as possible. But at this point, we didn't know much, like why it happened or how it happened; all we knew was that she died and that they weren't getting the baby sister they had waited so many months for.

What was a 20-minute drive went by so fast. I thought to myself, "Great! When you need time to go slow, it goes fast and when you need it to go fast, it takes forever."

And just like that, we pulled up into the driveway.

We decided to leave all our stuff in the car so as not to prolong the inevitable. After taking a few deep breaths again, we went in.

I went in first with Ross closely behind me. As I entered the living room, I saw Alexander sitting on the couch with his iPad. He looked up at me and immediately said, "Where were you guys? Why did you take so long to come back?" As he asked the question, he scanned my belly which he knew before he left was huge and I could see him processing that it was no longer as big. He also looked closely at my face which was clearly swollen from crying and looked sad.

Before he could process any more and ask anything else, I asked him where was Natalie to which he replied, "She's upstairs."

I put out my hand to hold his and said, "Ok. Come, Buddy, Daddy and I need to talk to you and your sister. Let's go upstairs and talk."

We got to our bedroom where we found Natalie on our bed watching her iPad. She sprung off the bed and screamed in jubilation, "Mummy, Daddy, you're home. I missed you so much!" She then ran into Ross' arms for a big hug, as she had been trained for months not to jump on me because of the baby.

We asked both kids to come sit on the bed with us. Alexander sat next to me and Natalie on Ross' lap.

Without hesitation I decided to just get to it.

I said, "We have some very sad news. While Eliana was in Mummy's tummy, something happened, and she got sick." I was now choked up and crying and could no longer speak.

Ross continued by saying, "This caused her heart to stop beating and well, you need your heart to beat and pump blood so you can be alive. And unfortunately, Eliana's heart was not beating so she died and is no longer coming home to be with us."

Alexander said loudly, with tears streaming down his face and now standing up, "WHAT do you mean she is not coming home? We've been so patient! We've been waiting for so long for her to come out! What do you mean she's not coming? This is the worst day ever!"

I couldn't argue with that; it *was* the worst day ever.

Alexander then started to cry a cry that sounded so similar to the cry I cried in the car. A cry I had never heard him cry before. The cry of a broken heart and a disappointment of a magnitude one shouldn't have to suffer at his tender age of 7. At this point, I was broken hearted for him and put out my arms to pull him over to hug him.

Crying as well, I said, "I know, Buddy, I'm so so sorry! I am so sad and disappointed too. I know you guys were waiting really really long and were so patient. I'm just so sorry."

We were all crying in a group huddle of sorts when out of nowhere, Natalie, with tears streaming down her face, says in an upbeat voice, "It's ok, guys. Eliana is in Heaven with God and Jesus is taking care of her. She's not sick anymore.

She's fine!" She then proceeded to jump off Ross' lap and back on to her bed to continue watching her iPad.

So caught off guard by her profound and very confident statement, we all stopped crying for a moment and looked over at her with a confused "what just happened" look.

Out of the mouths of babes, I suppose.

As things calmed down, I took a break and had a hot shower before bed. At the time, I found hot showers to be a quiet and healing retreat and after which I just felt physically better.

Just exhausted and ready for bed, the kids asked to sleep in bed with us. It was a long couple of days and though Ross and I were exhausted and needed a comfortable night's sleep that didn't include four people in one bed, we also needed the kids close as much as they needed us.

Of the two kids, Alexander was definitely taking it harder and was still visibly upset and crying. So, I hugged him tight and together we fell asleep.

Tomorrow was a new day and we were going to start it off as best we could together.

Aside: This was the hardest chapter to write and proofread. Being in this place emotionally pains me significantly. The whole experience in the hospital was hard, but this was the hardest part. I cried while writing every single word and I cried every time I had to proofread it. I cried the rest of the night after I wrote it and there was spillover emotionally of my mood that weekend I wrote it.

Chapter 7

F riday morning started the first day at home. I was the last to wake up. The house was quiet.

Though I could hear Alexander and Natalie downstairs, the house was deafeningly silent with the absence of the cries of a newborn. I naturally put my hand on my belly to rub it, only to notice the difference and that Eliana was gone from my physical person as well.

Just like that, she was gone and with her, all our plans, our dreams and our future as a family of five.

This was definitely not how I imagined our first morning at home from the hospital after giving birth. I let out a huge sigh as the reality of this very unexpected reality continued to set in.

In that moment, I noticed the bassinet that had been set up next to my bed a few weeks before was gone. It was quite heavy and I knew Lisa had a bad back, so I was wondering where it was and how it got there.

I headed down the hall toward the nursery / my home office and noticed the door was closed. Unless I was in a meeting, that door was never closed and I've really never seen it closed from the outside. It looked so strange to me. I opened the door and went in.

Though unfinished, the nursery was ready. Ready for us to change diapers on the beautiful changing table. Ready for Eliana to be in the crib so the kids could take a break from touching her. Ready to hang out while I was on a conference call or two. It was just ready and, honestly, just perfect. But there was no Eliana and she wasn't coming. The reality was painfully hard to reconcile.

How was this even possible?

How was this our reality?

How did we get here?

Hearing my footsteps upstairs, Ross came to check on me.

When he came in, we looked at each other. We both had pain in our eyes but tried to put on a brave face for the other. Here we were living in an alternate reality, one where Eliana was not with us, one we didn't expect, one that hurt so deeply.

That morning, our What's Apps and iMessages were going off like crazy with messages from family and friends checking in with us or sending condolences.

We also were receiving numerous calls from our very concerned parents, siblings and family stuck in Trinidad and Tobago and feeling helpless due to COVID lockdowns.

Though the calls kept coming in, I found it very hard to be on video calls because everyone I spoke to was crying. Honestly, if I could have dug myself a hole, crawled in and just hid in there forever, I would have. Dealing with everyone else's grief on top of my own, Ross' and the kids was unexpected and a challenge in an already hard situation.

I told my parents they could let our larger extended family know and Ross did the same for his side of the family. This was ultimately the opening of the floodgates of condolences and outpouring of love and concern from far and wide.

Ross and I spent most of the morning messaging people that we thought needed to know directly from us before the news from the others spread like wildfire.

I was so far along in my pregnancy with Eliana, literally due any day for at least a couple weeks, that it would be impossible for someone to see me not pregnant anymore and not assume we had a happy healthy baby at home.

The thought of having to correct someone and say it out loud just made me sick. This feeling stuck with me for weeks, if not months, after her death and every time I said it to someone, I couldn't stop the accompanying tears.

We planned to send the kids back to school on Monday and I was their main mode of transport. I just dreaded thinking I would go drop them off and have people assume the baby was born and happy and healthy at home. I dreaded having to say no and that she died; it would just be soul crushing. How was I going to solve this in order to protect my heart and not totally breakdown at school pick up?

I kept thinking I just needed as many people to know as possible to avoid this situation at all cost. I spoke to Ross about my concern and we decided I would post it to Social Media, once we made sure everyone who needed to know from us was told.

Though the nursery was empty, and I was saddened by that reality, I did find it comforting to be in there. It was the room I told Eliana was hers and where she could come. Part of me just wanted to sit there and hope her little spirit would show up and say hi. I sat in the bright green nursing chair I had used for Alexander and Natalie and planned to use for Eliana. It was still the most comfortable chair in the house and the only thing Eliana inherited from her siblings. We had not planned to have another baby after Natalie, so with the exception of strollers, we bought everything new for Eliana.

Taking a break from messages, Ross and I talked about what we needed to do that day. My car was still at the hospital, so that was one thing we needed to take care of. And we needed lunch. The kids loved The Yard House, so we made a plan to go there for lunch and then go pick up my car at the hospital.

As I walked downstairs to greet the kids, Natalie came up to me and touched my belly and said, "Mummy, Eliana is not in your belly anymore because she is dead." This was the first of many times 5-year-old Natalie's matter of fact way of talking about Eliana punched us in the gut with the cold hard truth.

I replied, "Yes, she's not in there anymore."

She then proceeded to say, "Well, if she's not in there anymore, you can just put another baby in there." She was so very proud of herself for providing what seemed like an easy fix to a big problem.

I said to her, "Peanut, it's not that easy."

Ross and I exchanged an 'OUCH, this is going to be interesting' look. Her simple way of thinking and trying to find a solution to our problem as a family was just that. Simple. Oh, to be a kid again where it could be that simple.

Lunch was a nice distraction. The kids were back to being happy, playing tic tac toe which removed some of the heaviness from the air around me. I tried to be as normal as I could be and even laughed a few times.

After lunch, we headed down to the hospital to get my car.

Once at the hospital, Natalie went with Ross in my car because of the TV and Alexander came with me.

While we were in the car waiting for Ross to clear the two days' worth of snow off my car, Alexander picked up on Natalie's comment from home and said to me, "Could we get a replacement baby? I won't care if it's a boy or a girl and we promise we will be patient and wait again. We know it will be a long wait but we will wait and be patient."

In that moment, I thought, "Geez, I think I replaced way too many broken toys; now they just think we can get a replacement baby."

I replied to him, "Buddy, it's not that simple and even so, if we were to have another baby, that baby would never replace Eliana. The experience you would have had with her would be different to the experience which you would have with another baby because they are different people with different personalities. So, it would never be exactly the same. One baby cannot replace another."

He then replied, "I know it wouldn't be exactly the same but I would still get to do all the things I planned to do with Eliana, like feed the baby, play with the baby, teach the baby how to walk and talk and spell."

He had a point. He would get to do all those things with a new baby, but it just was not that simple.

As we drove past the front of the hospital, Alexander asked if that was where everything happened and he asked me specifically what happened.

I explained to him what happened in the simplest way possible without sparing many details.

After I was done, I said, "You see, Buddy, what Mummy and Daddy went through at the hospital was really really hard and very sad. And well, we never want to go through that again. It's for this reason we cannot promise you a replacement baby. I do promise Mummy and Daddy will consider what you and your sister are asking for, but we need some time as we have a lot to process here and work through. Also, it needs to be a decision Mummy and Daddy make together. We have to agree so even if Mummy thinks she can do it again, Daddy may not agree because this was very very hard for Daddy too, and he never wants to go through this again as I'm sure you don't want to, either. I do promise if you give us some time, we will give you a final answer to this question and I hope you and Natalie can support us in whatever we decide, even if the answer is no. Can you agree to that?"

He said, "Yes, I will support you, whatever you decide, but I really hope we can get one."

In that moment, I felt like this was the first of many hard conversations on the horizon and I was definitely right.

Chapter 8

It was now Saturday at 12 PM and my aunt, uncle and cousin from Staten Island had arrived and I needed to go downstairs. They had asked the day before if they could come down to see us and bring some food. Although we were not up to receiving visitors, I said yes because my parents, at this point, were smothering us virtually with their excessive calls and messages of concern due to their constant worrying. Hence, I thought the visit necessary for everyone to calm down and give us the space we needed. A good report from my aunt and uncle that we were holding up as best as possible would hopefully solve this issue.

Thank God for hot showers. Once again, a shower helped me feel better. I proceeded downstairs to see everyone.

All the framed pictures for the funeral were in my shopping cart, but I was now worried about the delivery which said it would arrive Friday. I couldn't believe the fastest possible shipping would take that long to arrive.

I remember saying to everyone downstairs that had this happened in Trinidad, all these details with the funeral, all the issues with the framing and printing of the pictures would have been handled and we would have just had to pick songs and show up to the funeral because between Daddy, Mummy and Granny Moy, it would have been handled.

I expressed my concern over the pictures not arriving on time and everyone encouraged me to order them and have a backup plan in case they didn't arrive. They were right. So I paid for the shopping cart and hoped for the best.

Despite not wanting visitors, it was good to see family as we were able to talk and laugh a bit. We had an especially good laugh when Ross had an allergic reaction to a weird candy he bought the day before in CVS. He was so protective of the sour apple flavored candy which was making him have a coughing fit and choke determined not to see his money and candy be thrown out. He was ready to go dumpster diving for it, after I threw it in the trash in a dramatic attempt to save his life. So funny! God knew we needed a good laugh.

It was now 2:30 PM and we needed to go to the funeral home to make arrangements for the funeral and to see Eliana for the first time since leaving the hospital on Thursday, just two days before.

We said goodbye to our family and dropped the kids off to their friends' house for a play date.

The funeral home was nice, well, as nice as funeral homes go, I suppose. We went up the grand staircase and into the conference room where we met the funeral home owner and his intern.

So many details and decisions. I felt totally overwhelmed.

One thing in particular caused me the most stress throughout that whole conversation.

We had chosen the date for the funeral to be Saturday, February 27, as it would allow most of our family and friends who worked during the week to attend Eliana's funeral virtually. This was very important to us. However, the funeral director indicated if we had the funeral on a weekend, it wouldn't be possible for us to attend the cremation as the crematorium does not allow family viewings after 12 PM on the weekend.

This would mean our only option would be to have the funeral on Saturday and have her wait to be cremated on Monday so we could attend.

This was a huge problem for me.

At this point in the discussion, Ross made it clear he didn't want to see her casket go into the fire, so not going to the crematorium on Saturday was ok for him.

Very upset, I said loudly, "I do not want to have the funeral be over and have her ushered out in the casket and then go in the car and I wave her off like she's leaving at the airport. I need a moment to say goodbye and I need to take her to the crematorium myself. I cannot have her go alone."

The funeral director could see how much this was upsetting me and said, "So, what I am hearing is that you are ok with not seeing the casket go into the fire but would like to drive over with the casket and escort her to the crematorium where you can have a moment to say your goodbyes."

I said, "Yes, that's what I want." I was finally feeling heard and understood.

He then said, "Well, that is totally reasonable and we can arrange that. The only thing is that once at the crematorium, they will not be able to open the casket again."

I then asked him if we could have a private viewing for a few family members and close friends before the funeral as well as for us to spend some extra time with her and say goodbye with the casket open.

He replied, indicating there was another funeral that morning so the only room available would be a small room upstairs.

I agreed this would work because we were not having a lot of people attend this part.

We then talked urns, caskets, flowers, obituaries, payment and so on, so many decisions. At this point in my life, I had definitely thought the first time I would be making these types of decisions or be present for a conversation like this would be for the death of a parent or in-law Unfortunately, this wasn't the case.

Finally, it was over and they could take us down to see Eliana.

Back together again. She looked different from the hospital but the same. She was definitely frozen and cold.

It was very hard for Ross to see her like this. He had only ever seen one dead body before which was my best friend Natalie, nine years prior. So unfortunately for him, the second dead body he ever saw was his child which made it understandably very difficult.

For me, I had been seeing dead bodies from the age of five when I attended my great grandmother's funeral and then after that, my maternal grandfather's funeral when I was ten, in addition to countless other people's funerals and wakes including Natalie's and my paternal grandfather's years later.

So dead bodies didn't bother me as much. In the case of Eliana, just seeing her little body gave me so much comfort.

We didn't spend very long with her because I could see it was upsetting Ross to be there, but he was just staying for me because I needed to see her. When I asked him what was wrong and if he wanted to leave, he said it just hurt him too much to see her like that and that I could do what I needed to do for me but he didn't want to see her again like that, so he won't be coming back with me.

As we left, I asked the funeral director if I would be able to come back to see her on Monday. He expressed concern about her body decomposing faster by them taking her in and out of the freezer. He explained that for them to have her out for us to see her that day, they had taken her out earlier that morning so she wouldn't be as cold.

I told him very pragmatically, "You don't need to take her out early to thaw her out. I understand. She's dead and frozen; it makes no difference to me. I just need you to take her out just before I arrive and put her back in when I leave. This way, we can preserve her body as best as possible and I get to see her, which is something that I need."

He agreed and we arranged for me to come back on Monday at 12 PM. This gave me something to look forward to. I'll see her again on Monday.

We found out later on in conversation with the Funeral home owner that his son was a twin and he and his wife lost their other son as an infant; thus, he empathized deeply with our loss.

Ross and I went home before picking up the kids to see if we could find an outfit for Eliana to be changed into for the funeral and her cremation. Another very frustrating task.

I had wanted to find a beautiful white christening gown for my beautiful girl but found it to be challenging to find in her size. After searching and searching online, I finally found something I loved, complete with the gown, shoes and hat. Success! I placed the order.

Within thirty minutes of placing the order, I received a call from the company I ordered it from. The customer service representative indicated she noticed I selected overnight shipping and that due to the storm in Texas, they couldn't guarantee it would be delivered in time. As a result, she offered me the opportunity to cancel. Hesitantly, I agreed and she cancelled the order quickly before I changed my mind and said "no, keep the order."

Now I had no dress. And the stock on the site didn't refresh so I couldn't reorder it. I was beyond frustrated and kept looking and looking online. Never before had online shopping been so painful and hard.

On top of this frustration, my breasts were now causing me a lot of pain, so I told Ross we needed cabbage. He said confused, "cabbage?" I replied, "Yeah, apparently, it's supposed to stop breastmilk. It's literally written on the paper from the hospital, and I've heard about it through my mama's group." We had a laugh about the cabbage.

As we were in the nursery when all this was happening, Ross decided to open the purple keepsake box the hospital gave us. There he found the pictures the kind nurses took. Looking through the pictures, he said, "Geez, these pictures are horrible! Could they have made her look anymore dead? I never want to see these pictures again. Thank God we took our own."

I said, "Let me see."

He said, "Are you sure? They are pretty bad."

Confident they couldn't be that bad, I put out my hand for the pics. As I started to review them, I realized he was very right. I laughed and said, "Oh my, you are right. They are horrible; we should burn them. I really hope that the other family who was there took their own pics because could you imagine if we didn't and we were depending on these pictures and came home and this is all we had? Thank God we took our own."

We were never more grateful for the 211 pictures and four videos taken of our precious Angel as we were in that moment.

On Saturday night, we had a late night due to a cautionary trip to the OB triage at the hospital because of concerns about my postpartum bleeding. Getting home at 2:30 AM, we were exhausted. The trip to the hospital was warranted, but it did take forever, as hospital visits usually do.

I woke up exhausted and frustrated because the dress for Eliana still was not available. Crying again, poor Ross woke up and asked what was wrong.

I said, crying, "I cannot keep her alive. I cannot bury her properly. I'm just so useless."

Ross said, "Let me help you. Show me what you like and let me see if I can find it." After a bit of searching, Ross says "What about this?" The gown was from the same designer on a different site, but it was a unisex outfit, so not very girly. After looking at it some more, I appreciated the champagne-colored trim and it did come with a hat and shoes.

Ross then said to me, "Why do you need the shoes?" I shot him a look and before I could say anything, he said quickly, "Buy whatever you think is necessary."

We placed the order and it was done. Thank God for Ross and for small mercies because I was so defeated in that moment.

Unfortunately, that day those feelings of defeat, frustration and overwhelming grief were all over me. It felt like weights were tied to my feet and I was dropped in the deep end of a pool and struggling to keep my head above water.

I started to replay the weeks and doctors' visits prior to February 17.

How did this happen!?

How did I not know something was wrong!?

I recalled the last NST (non-stress test) the week before when she took twenty minutes to get her movements in, but I also didn't have lunch before I went in and they had no apple juice, so it wasn't a huge shock.

I then recalled the machine beeping out of control when she hit 170 on the heart monitor when making her accelerated movement. She had never been higher than 158, so this had alarmed me and I voiced my concerns to the high-risk doctor, the nurse and the OB. Everyone said it was normal and nothing to be concerned about.

I also thought back to the week before when I voiced concern again to the high-risk doctor, nurse and OB saying I thought her movement for her as an individual had decreased, but I was told she was still moving well within range, so there was nothing to worry about.

I thought back even further, voicing concerns about her kidney fluid and whether we should take her out early, to which they indicated the best place for her was in my womb. If she came out and needed surgery, she needed to be as far along as possible. I knew this personally to be true and nothing to worry about because Natalie had the same issue in utero and Eliana was stable, not getting worse but also not getting better.

I could feel myself getting angry. Angry at myself for not advocating enough for her. Angry for not making the doctors hear and take my concerns more seriously. Angry that the doctors didn't do more or listen to me. I could feel I was going to a place I did not want to go.

My mom called around that time and, coincidentally, echoed my angry feelings regarding the doctors. I told her I needed to hang up.

Now I was at a crossroads again. Was I going to call my Lawyer friend Mel or was I going to call my neonatologist friend Georsan? Both these friends I have known since I was twelve years old and I knew I could call them in this situation for support.

Quickly thinking through the options and where I wanted to be in terms of peace, I called Georsan. I walked her through every detail of my pregnancy. She had actually known most of the details previously as I had been consulting with her and other doctor friends throughout. But this time, I walked her through every last detail running through my mind.

At the end of the detailed run through and after explaining why certain things happen like the machine beeping when she hit 170, Georsan said to me, "The friend in me so badly wants to tell you that you were right, but the professional in me has to tell you that based on everything you have told me, I would not have advised you any differently. There was nothing you or the doctors could have done. I'm sorry."

If there was ever a professional opinion I have always trusted, especially when it comes to my children's health, it is Georsan's and I knew she would be straight with me.

Looking back on it now, I believe God knew I needed a friend like her for this moment and put her in my life from age twelve and bonded us to be inseparable through our shared love for Natalie when she had died nine years earlier.

This wouldn't be the first or last time I called upon Georsan to walk me off the ledge.

My mom called back not long after and I said to her, "I spoke to Georsan; she would not have advised anything differently and that is enough for me. I know you are angry and grieving too, but I cannot be in that place of anger. It's just not an emotion I can have in my space, so you cannot call me if that's an emotion you cannot control." It was a hard line to take, but I needed to preserve the little sanity I had left.

Trying to make things as normal as possible for the kids, we decided to go to their standing tennis lesson that day. This was a welcomed and helpful distraction. While sitting at tennis, I multitasked by writing Eliana's obituary and setting up the St. Jude's donations page. We appreciated all the flowers and bereavement gifts that kept coming but also wanted to redirect these kind gestures to something that would help others not suffer this same way. St Jude's was the best we could think of at the time. Thanks to the generosity of so many family members, friends and colleagues, we raised over $2000 for St. Jude's in Memory of our little Angel, Eliana.

After tennis, we went to lunch at Zoe's as we wanted to feed the kids something more than pizza. As we sat down to eat, another thought came to my mind (the devil now working overtime to derail me). I started to think about the Saturday before Eliana died. Ross and I went to dinner with Natalie at the club after her Spa-ty (Spa Party) and I had had cooked oysters as an appetizer. I knew raw oysters were a big no during pregnancy but that cooked ones were ok. I said to Ross quietly, "What if I ate the oysters last weekend and killed her." Immediately I started to cry.

He said to me, "Babe, why are you doing this to yourself?"

I said, "If the test results come back and say it was the oysters, I will lose my mind. I will never be able to forgive myself. I just won't be able to handle it."

The next day at the funeral home, while visiting Eliana, the results for the Toxoplasmosis came to my phone. Trying to interpret them myself, I started to google (bad idea). One of the numbers on the test was sky high and I immediately went into a tailspin. Eliana was dead in front of me and the results as I was reading them told me it was the oysters and my fault. A stupid food decision by me killed her, making me the worse type of mother. At this point, I was crying and apologizing to her uncontrollably. Through my tears, I messaged Georsan a screen shot of the results with a message saying, It was the oysters. I killed her and it was all my fault!"

Georsan called me immediately and said, "First of all, I am not sure why you are even being allowed to get test results without interpretation; that is just not productive in this situation. Also is this the only Toxso results you got? They usually come in pairs."

She was right; it did come in a pair. I screen shotted the other result which I totally ignored because the number was low.

Georsan then said, "Ok. Well, it was not the oysters and you did not kill her." She went on to say, "The high number you are looking at indicates that a very very long time ago, you did have toxoplasmosis and this is the level of antibodies you have for it. The other number on other test means that you have not had a recent infection and therefore, it could not have been the oysters or toxoplasmosis. You did not kill her. I have treated babies with toxoplasmosis and they appear swollen. Eliana was perfect and definitely not swollen."

I finally started to breathe again. Thank God, it wasn't the oysters.

Things were getting out of control and I knew it was because I was not praying enough. Over the years, I have found when I am not praying the Rosary every day and especially through difficult times, things spiral out of control.

Aunt Lisa had actually said to me that morning I needed to pray for Eliana, even though she was in Heaven and I believe this was a direct message from God, telling me pray for her because He knew I would do anything for her, including pray.

That day, I sat in the car outside of the funeral home and prayed the Rosary for the first time since Eliana died, the first time in five days which was a long time for me. So many people were praying for our family but I was not praying for myself or for Eliana.

After praying, I headed over to school to pick up the kids. It was my first school pick up since Eliana died and I needed as much strength as possible; drop off was really hard that morning. I also needed as much strength as possible to get through the rest of the day.

After praying the Rosary that day, I truly felt my connection with the Holy Spirit return, my calm and sense of peace returned. Things stopped spinning out of control. I was back in the presence of the Lord and in a state of Grace. The grief was still very much present, but I was being comforted by the only one capable of providing the comfort at the level I needed to survive.

This was my answer. I knew it all along but fought it. But now, I saw no other option. It was critical to my survival. It was clear now the Rosary was my lifeline as it had been so many times before and this time I would be holding on for dear life.

Chapter 9

The drive to school Tuesday morning started off like any other by practicing Alexander's spelling words for his Friday test. I asked Alexander to spell the word little, to which he replied, "L-I-T-T-L-E little."

He then used it in a sentence saying, "Our little sister."

Natalie then quickly jumped in and added, "Our little sister is dead."

I thought to myself, "Oh my, here we go."

Alexander then responded to Natalie, "Yes, she is dead, but her spirit is alive in Heaven."

Natalie then says combatively, "Yes, but she is still dead."

I quickly intervened as they were headed for a full-blown argument over who was right. I said, "All these statements are true and can be true at the same time, making everyone right. Yes, she is your little sister, yes, she is dead and yes, she is alive in spirit in Heaven." They both accepted and agreed that everyone was right.

Alexander then said, "Mummy, why would Jesus want Eliana in Heaven with Him so soon after she was born?"

These were the tough questions I knew would eventually come as they started to truly process the loss of their sister.

In that moment, all I could do was answer from my heart as best as I understood and believed. I said, "Well, Buddy, we are all here on earth to either learn lessons or serve a purpose to impact the lives of others or both. Once that has been completed, Jesus calls us back to Heaven to be with Him for our eternal life. In Eliana's case, her purpose was fulfilled, and Jesus called her back to Heaven to be with Him. You see, this is all part of God's plan and God makes the best plans. God's plans are so big we cannot comprehend at our level all the parts of His plan. Also, in some cases like with Eliana, we may never know why this was part of God's plan and honestly, it's not for us to know but it is for us to accept. Maybe one day when Mummy goes to Heaven, God will tell me why but even then, He may choose not to and I may never know why and that's ok. It is important to understand that for us to truly accept God's plan, we cannot be angry or bitter. We can be sad but not angry because that would mean we don't truly accept or have faith this is His plan. Also, because you don't know when you will be called back to Jesus, you must always be ready to go which is why we must try to live a good life here on earth by being kind and helping others and not doing things that would keep us out of Heaven, so when our time comes and Jesus calls us to Heaven, we can go straight up without any pit stops and see Eliana and Aunty Natalie as soon as we get there."

I then asked the kids if they understood what I was trying to say and surprisingly, they said yes.

After dropping the kids off at school and talking to a close friend about the conversation I had with the kids that morning, I headed home, feeling in a place of peace.

As 12 PM approached, I decided to join my office Rosary group to pray the Rosary with them for the first time since Eliana died.

Everyone asked how I was doing. I explained that the past six days had been very hard and that the only thing holding me together at that point was my faith.

As I said that, Velia, the retiree of our group, said to me, "Candace, I am so proud of you. Thank God for your faith." She then said to me, "Do you remember when you joined the Rosary group?"

I replied, "Yes. It was during lent years ago. We had received many blessings the year before and it was one of three promises I made to God in thanksgiving for all the blessings we received the prior year. I had promised God the kids would always go to Catholic school once we could afford it, that we would build a prayer garden dedicated to the Virgin Mary once we moved into our "home" whenever that was and that I would go to Rosary group for lent. I started Rosary group that lent and never stopped going."

The ladies laughed and said, "Yes, remember where you were sitting in the office just outside the conference room where we prayed; we would always invite you to join us but you never came then you left us and your convenient location to move to a new office across the street having to walk 10 mins in order to join us years later."

Velia then said to me, "I remember the day you joined us. It was an Ash Wednesday, and I never forgot the look on your face the first time you led (a decade of the Rosary). You led the 3rd Glorious Mystery Descent of the Holy Spirit and your face just lit up as you read it. This was before we realized we should be doing the Sorrowful throughout lent." She laughed.

WOW! She was right! I did join Rosary group on Ash Wednesday. I started to think back how many years ago it was.

In that moment, the connection to Ash Wednesday struck me in the most undeniable way. All of a sudden, things started to come into focus and be revealed by the

Lord, revealed in a way that can only happen when you are lifted up from the weeds to have a bird's eye view.

I started praying the Rosary in Rosary group three to five times per week at work four years prior on Ash Wednesday and never stopped. That promise of thanksgiving to God for all my blessings received in 2016 started my journey to strengthening my faith to the point it could hold me up now. Fast forward to four years later when my biggest test of faith started with the stopping of Eliana's heart somewhere between 12 AM and 7 PM on Ash Wednesday.

For years, I have walked through my life believing through and through there are no coincidences in life, only miracles, big and small. The mere connection of these occurrences and the revelation itself was a miracle which had me speechless.

Within three hours of my conversation with the kids where I truly in my heart accepted this was God's plan and through my faith didn't need to know why, God revealed to me this was, indeed, His plan and by so doing, this opened my heart and ears to seek and learn the purpose.

After Rosary group that day, I was profoundly uplifted by the Ash Wednesday connection and thought to myself that though this situation was devastatingly hard, God loved me enough to equip me with the strengthening of my faith over the past four years so I could survive the loss of Eliana. I was grateful, humbled and in a good place, which helped as I was headed to pick up the kids from school to take them to the funeral home to see Eliana for the first time.

Chapter 10

The day before, on Monday afternoon while doing homework with Alexander, I continued to feel the weight of Eliana's loss on the kids.

How was this going to affect their future?

Alexander, who without a doubt is my sensitive child, has always been deeply affected by disappointments in general and for this reason, he was especially on my mind. I thought to myself, all those months of the kids waiting and bonding with her and because of COVID, they were not even able to come to the hospital to see her. They never got to see what she looked like in real life, other than in the pictures I showed them. They never got to touch her and know that the person they were poking in my belly was real.

This made me sad.

Ross and I had discussed briefly on the previous Saturday when we saw Eliana at the funeral home whether we should take the kids to see her and decided against it, thinking it would somehow make it worse. However, the more I thought about it, the more my instincts told me I should not make the choice for them. They were old enough to decide for themselves, Alexander being seven and Natalie being five.

In that moment, I decided to pose the question to both kids. I explained that I wanted to give them the opportunity to go meet Eliana at the funeral home. And although going to see her wouldn't change the fact she was dead or the fact that she wasn't coming home, they would be able to meet her, see her and touch her. I showed them a picture of what she looked like on Saturday which was the same when I visited her on Monday so they would not be surprised. I explained that I wanted them to decide for themselves what they wanted to do and assured them I wouldn't be mad if they said no but they needed to decide because after Saturday, they wouldn't have the opportunity again.

Natalie right away said, "Yes, I want to go see her!"

I then turned to Alexander who I could tell was seriously thinking about it.

I said, "Buddy, you do not have to go because you think I want you to go or because you think it will make me happy. You can say no."

He nodded, still thinking about it and then said tentatively, "I want to go."

I asked him if he was sure, and he reassured me more confidently by saying, "Yes, I'm sure. I want to meet her." I then said to both kids, "Ok. Well, I'll make the arrangements and we will go after school tomorrow (Tuesday) and let me know if you change your mind before then."

As we got into the car after school pick up, I said to the kids, "Ok, we are going to go to funeral home to see Eliana. You can still change your mind if you don't want to go. Are you sure you still want to go?" They both said yes and asked how long it would take to get there. I replied, "Not long. It's like ten minutes away, close to Ava's Daddy's pizza place."

When we arrived at the funeral home, I explained that we would be going into a special room with Eliana and that they would be able to touch her but needed to be gentle.

As we entered the funeral home, the kids said hello to the gentleman that let us in. He seemed surprised I was coming in with two kids to see a dead baby. The kids were actively looking around and commented on how nice it was and that they liked the fake fireplace. We were escorted to the small room and were given time alone with Eliana.

Honestly, I was a little nervous how they were going to react, so I went in first and pulled up a stool so they would be able to sit by the table. I then said, "It's ok. Come and see her." Natalie came and sat on my lap but didn't say anything.

Alexander then came in slowly.

As he laid eyes on Eliana for the first time, he said, "Aww, Mummy, you were right; she does look like me." It was the most beautiful statement. Honestly, I did not expect that reaction at all, but somehow Alexander was able to look past her deep dark red face and see her as I saw her—just beautiful.

I said, smiling widely at him, "I told you she did! She looks just like you when you were a baby."

Then he said, "Except I think she has Natalie's eyebrows."

He then sat right next to her and just stared for a while. After a couple minutes, he asked me if he could touch her and I said, "Yes you can but she's going to be a little cold." As he touched his little sister face gently, he turned to me and said, "Mummy, I am so happy I came; I am so happy I got to meet her." In that moment, I knew I made the right choice.

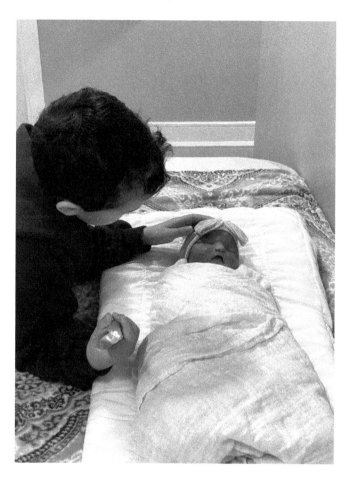

Natalie, on the other hand, was on my lap, quiet and holding on very tight. When I asked her if she was ok, she indicated she was a little scared. Springing into true big brother mode, Alexander said to her, "Natalie, it's ok, there is nothing to be scared of. Come and touch her cheek; it's very soft. Her nose, too." She proceeded off my lap and inched closer to Alexander to touch Eliana's cheek. She then said, "You're right. It is soft and a little cold and her little nose is bouncy and not so cold."

Alexander then asked why she was so cold. So, I explained that once a person dies, their body starts to break down and cannot be preserved without going into a very cold freezer, so technically she's frozen. I then said that is why after Saturday you won't be able to come see her because we need to cremate her body as it cannot stay like this forever.

Alexander then asked what cremation was. So, I explained that when someone dies because their body cannot last, you have to decide to either bury them in a cemetery or cremate them.

"Cremating a body is like burning wood." I explained. "When you burn wood, it turns to ashes and when you burn a body, the same thing happens; it turns to ashes." I explained further, "Because Mummy and Daddy do not know if we would be in New Jersey forever, we didn't want to bury Eliana in a cemetery here and then move and leave her behind. So, we decided to cremate her so her ashes can be at home with us until Mummy dies, hopefully a long time from now, and she can be buried with me, or we move to Trinidad she can go to our family plot in the cemetery there."

After answering all their questions, I asked the kids if they would be willing to have a picture taken of the four of us, which they happily agreed. I propped my phone on top of a box of tissues and picked up Eliana to cradle her. Using the photo timer, I was able to capture a few pictures of me and my three babies.

What a gift, given the circumstances!

As the time approached 4 PM. I told the kids that we needed to leave as the funeral home was closing. I told them I was coming back tomorrow by myself while they were in school and that they would see Eliana again on Saturday. With tears in their eyes, they said, "No, Mummy, we want to come back tomorrow with you; we want to come back and see her again."

I knew the feeling and the comfort her little body gave me, so I agreed they could come back again the next day.

As we sat in the Mc Donald's drive through line, I thought back to what had just happened at the funeral home with the kids. I felt so grateful for that moment and for that picture of me and my three babies I thought I would never have.

Thank God for small mercies.

Chapter 11

I spent most of Wednesday preparing for the funeral by choosing readings and songs as Father Jack was coming to our house later that evening to go through everything. This was not an easy task and listening to all the song options overwhelmed me and made me feel very emotional. Ross had been back to work since Monday and had vetoed a couple song choices the night before, though he said to choose whatever I wanted.

Looking forward to seeing Eliana with the kids again, I headed over to the school to pick them up. The day before had gone so well and had really uplifted me, so I had high hopes for that day's visit. However, I was acutely aware that my mood was not great with all the funeral preparations hanging over me.

I hurried the kids after school pick up so we could get to the funeral home earlier than the previous day and have more time to spend with her before they closed at 4 PM.

Once we got into the room with Eliana, the kids were happy to see her again. They played with her for a few minutes, but the novelty from the day before had worn off. After just five minutes, they both began to complain they were hungry and asked when we were going to leave (usual kid stuff). I agreed to order pizza and told them we would pick it up when we left but that it would take the pizza 15-20 minutes to be made so we would just stay here with Eliana until the pizza was ready.

Eventually, after spending just twenty minutes there, I said, "Fine. Let's go" because of the excessive whining. I then said in a very annoyed tone, "I am coming back tomorrow by myself. You will see her on Saturday because there is limited time and you just wasted my time today."

I felt bad for being so annoyed with them as I knew they were just being kids and honestly, she was dead, so there really wasn't much for them to do. Feeling bad in the car, I explained to them that given the situation and cremation being on Saturday, I only had a little bit of time with Eliana left and that made me very sad. I explained I would have liked to spend an hour there today and know that's a long time for them to just sit there. So Mummy would prefer to go there tomorrow by myself so I could spend the whole hour with their sister. After my calmer explanation, they agreed I should go alone the next day and apologized for rushing me to leave.

The whole situation that afternoon, as well as the funeral preparations, upset me a lot as I realized that my time with her little body which was giving me so much comfort was coming to an end. How was I going to manage after Saturday? I was totally dreading it.

That night, after Father Jack left, I was talking to Ross when another thought occurred to me. In that moment, I realized I never saw her with her hat off. I had never seen the beautiful full head of hair that the ultrasound techs talked about. I verbalized this to Ross. He said, "You did see her with her hat off when she just came out; you even commented about it." I said, "I did? I can barely remember. I don't even know what her hands or feet look like because she was swaddled the whole time in the hospital and when I went to look, you told me not to. I shouldn't have listened to you because what you are able to stomach is different from me."

I knew it wasn't his fault and I was just really upset with myself for listening to him.

I went to sleep crying that night because now I regretted that decision to not inspect her little body from head to toe and commit it to memory. It pained me to my core. How could I not know what her little hands and feet looked like? How did I not know what her little tummy or belly button looked like? How could I never have held her hand, touched her fingers or her toes before? I could feel the grief overwhelming me and swallowing me up.

Thursday morning, I had planned to go to the funeral home at 12 PM, but I called to push back the time to 1:30 PM as I was looking for the perfect swaddle for Saturday. The outfit we purchased online had arrived, but the neckline seemed lower than expected. She had a significant birth wound on the right side of her neck, resulting in a large piece of skin missing. With close family and friends coming to view her little body at the funeral home before the service, I wanted her, though dead, to look her best. Albeit, when I dropped off the outfit the day before, I had discussed with the Funeral Director this very concern and indicated I would prefer to swaddle her for the private viewing, should the outfit not suffice. He agreed I could come early on Saturday morning, and we could make a game time decision on the swaddle.

Now, I was rushing about all morning trying to find the perfect muslin swaddle. My gut (aka the Holy Spirit) had told me go to Target, but I ignored the advice and went to BuyBuy Baby instead.

Oh, why did I not listen! BuyBuy Baby was absolutely torture. The usual intoxicating baby smell was now like a slow acting poison crushing my heart. Compounding this pain was the location of the blankets which was in the back of the baby girl clothing section. The whole experience pained me physically and I couldn't get out of there fast enough. In full self-preservation mode, I told myself to just buy all the possible options on the shelf and leave.

$150 worth of blankets and socks later, I was back in the car crying. That was so hard, and I didn't even really like anything I found. I should have listened to the Holy Spirit and not gone in there, but I didn't.

After my best friend Natalie died in 2011, one of my main outlets for my grief was skiing. We literally skied every weekend that season after Natalie died because every waking moment was spent replaying our last interaction when I said goodbye to her in ICU in Trinidad. I knew that day that though I told her I would be back, deep down she and I both knew she wasn't going to make it; it would be our last time together. The guilt of leaving my friend that day was on constant replay in my mind 24/7, haunting me for months, whether I was awake or asleep. Skiing for me during that time provided me with short breaks while coming down the mountain as each run would require a lot of concentration to avoid my falling.

Now all these years later, with Eliana's death so fresh, I wished to retreat to the mountains again. I had told Ross earlier that week that I needed to go skiing and that the level of grief I was grappling with would require a really big mountain. I said seeing that we did not have a newborn and I was no longer pregnant, I didn't see why we couldn't get on a plane and go to Colorado. Very serious about my need for a ski trip in the near future, I put my skis in the car to drop them off to be waxed and tuned at the ski shop which was close to BuyBuy Baby.

The trip to BuyBuy Baby had left me in a mess, but I also wanted to drop my skis off. So, I did my best to compose myself and headed over to the ski shop. With my eyes swollen from crying, I walked into the ski shop to drop off my skis. I was greeted by one of the young guys working there. I said, "I came to drop off my skis to be waxed and tuned." I think he could tell I was a bit under the weather and not knowing why I was upset and the fact I still looked pregnant a week postpartum, he tried to make a joke by saying, "Are the skis for you or the baby." I just pretended to laugh and nodded as I was trying to hold back my tears.

After filling out the paperwork, a concerned older lady asked if she could check me out at the other register. When we got there, she said to me, "You look like you are having a rough day." I nodded and remained quiet as I was not able to speak. She asked, "Is there anything I can do to help you?" With tears rolling down and hitting my mask, I shook my head no. I was touched by her concern and kindness, but I couldn't talk about it so I paid for the skis and a bottle of maple syrup and left.

As way of background, over the past five years I had built an active connection with God through the Holy Spirit where I get "messages", "confirming thoughts" or "direction" through random occurrences with number sequences, billboards, signs, license plates, bumper stickers, street signs, butterflies, things people say or people messaging me out of the blue or songs that speak to me in certain moments. At first, I thought these were just mere coincidences, but when it started happening a lot on big and small things and I would follow the "guidance or nudge," I realized it was meant for me to take notice and be guided accordingly. For example, one time I was about to sign a lease for an apartment in NYC and happened to look down on my phone and noticed 666 on my inbox. In that moment, I stopped immediately and told the person I needed to think about it. Soon after leaving that apartment building, while on the sidewalk, an agent called me and said he had an apartment uptown to show me. What was strange about this call was I never reached out to this agent directly, but somehow, he had my contact info and called just as I needed an almost immediate solution. I asked if he could show me the apartment right away as I needed to see it ASAP with only three hours in the city before I needed to catch the bus home and head straight to the airport. That day, I followed where the Holy Spirit led me and signed the lease immediately after viewing the apartment. The apartment was exactly where God wanted us. It was much bigger than the other place, in a great neighborhood on the Upper East Side, in a family friendly building and within walking distance to St. Stephen of Hungary School where Alexander would attend PK3.

I recall another time while I was driving to the bus at 5 AM during the first week of starting my daily 4-hour round trip commute to NYC for work. I was crying, saying, "Lord, I know You wanted us to move here, but I just can't do this. It's so hard." Then out of nowhere, the Lauren Daigle song "Trust in me" came streaming over Amazon music. In that moment, as I looked up with tears in my eyes, I saw a billboard with a white dove saying, *Jesus is the way Pray* on the side of the highway. So, I did. The following week, my supervisor, who was on maternity leave, returned to the office and announced she would be working two days from home. This meant I could do it, too. Now I work mostly from home, something I never thought possible when we moved here almost three years ago. We took a massive leap of faith and moved to South Jersey because God led us here.

Anyway, after leaving the ski shop, I was crying a lot again but started driving as I needed to get to the funeral home to see Eliana at 1:30 PM. In that moment, I was crying because I was just feeling so totally defeated by the weight of everything. I knew it was God's plan and I accepted it, but I still felt like I was drowning in my grief. I had prayed the Rosary on my way down to BuyBuy Baby so I decided to put on Lauren Daigle on Amazon music and hit shuffle to see what song would come on. I was essentially begging God to speak to me. For years, Trust in Me has been the song that would come randomly on shuffle that would calm my worries but not this time. The song Rescue began playing and literally every word spoke to everything I was feeling in that moment and God was saying He was hearing me.

I recommend you listen to it to truly understand what a lifeline this song was to me in that moment. The fact that it came on randomly on shuffle is no coincidence.

Rescue - Lauren Daigle
Songwriters: Jason David Ingram / Lauren Daigle / Paul
Brendon Mabury

You are not hidden
There's never been a moment
You were forgotten
You are not hopeless
Though you have been broken
Your innocence stolen

I hear you whisper underneath your breath
I hear your SOS, your SOS

I will send out an army to find you
In the middle of the darkest night
It's true, I will rescue you
There is no distance
That cannot be covered
Over and over
You're not defenseless
I'll be your shelter
I'll be your armor

I hear you whisper underneath your breath
I hear your SOS, your SOS

I will send out an army to find you
In the middle of the darkest night
It's true, I will rescue you
I will never stop marching to reach you
In the middle of the hardest fight
It's true, I will rescue you

*I hear the whisper underneath your breath
I hear you whisper, you have nothing left
I will send out an army to find you
In the middle of the darkest night
It's true, I will rescue you
I will never stop marching to reach you
In the middle of the hardest fight
It's true, I will rescue you*

Oh, I will rescue you[1]

[1] "Rescue Lyrics by Lauren Daigle" Source: Musixmatch. https://g.co/
kgs/9KrYjJ

Chapter 12

I arrived at the funeral home feeling a little bit better after listening to Rescue in the car. God was hearing me; I was not alone; I was in a place of Grace.

Seeing Eliana always made me feel better, even on my toughest days and today was no different.

I went in there determined to at least try to inspect her from head to toe. She had been dead for a week and swaddled so I was very nervous what un-swaddling her might reveal. But I had to do it, even if I would end up regretting it later.

I slowly and gently unwrapped her swaddle.

As I opened the swaddle and all was revealed, I thought to myself, "OH MY WORD! What a horrible outfit! The outfit was literally the hospital's version of a christening hospital gown with an open back.

Fortunately, her outfit was the only bad thing in the swaddle.

I felt like I was seeing her for the first time.

First, I touched her little hands and fingers.

Since her cheeks were frozen solid, I had expected her hands to be frozen solid, too. However, other than being a little cold, they were soft beautiful baby hands which I delighted in holding and playing with.

What a gift!

As she was cold in the hospital too, her hands were just the same as they would have been a week earlier.

Thank God for small mercies.

Looking closer at her hands and arms, I noticed her wrists were blue with Mongolian Blue spots, just like Natalie when she was born. I told her just like Natalie, those blue wrists would have faded had she lived.

As I looked at her forearms, I noticed she had a lot of fine little black hairs, more than Alexander and Natalie for sure. I also noticed she had a blue birthmark on her right forearm just like Natalie has on her right hand. Despite all the similarities to Natalie, her face looked so much like Alexander.

Eliana turned out to be a beautiful mix of her siblings.

I eventually proceeded to her little feet and legs. Just like her hands, her feet were not frozen. They were perfect. She definitely, like her siblings, had Ross' toenails. Her feet were beautiful soft baby feet. Her little legs were long, thin and floppy.

I took pictures and videos of my sweet Angel, determined not to forget anything.

Thanking God for His continued mercies, I was so grateful for this second chance.

I continued to scan her entire body for more distinguishing marks but could not find anything else.

She did, however, have a lot of birth scars and battle wounds which made me feel more assured that we made the right decision to not do the autopsy. Her little body had definitely been through a lot.

Eventually, I moved up to her head. With the hat on, I could feel a large soft spot toward the back, so I was so unsure what would happen if I tried to remove her hat.

Slowly and gently, I removed her hat to reveal a full head of beautiful black wavy hair. It was amazing that without her hat, she was no longer Alexander's twin but totally had her own look. Seeing all her hair made me smile as I recalled every single Ultrasound Technician saying the exact same thing, "Whoa, she's got a lot of hair!"

Before swaddling her back up, I decided that though I couldn't change her outfit, I would at least put on some nice newborn socks; the knitted socks the hospital dressed her in were huge and I felt that her beautiful feet deserved some proper socks.

With her new socks on, I swaddled her back up and put back on her hat.

My time with her that day flew by, but I was feeling so much better by the end of that visit because I no longer had that regret hanging over me.

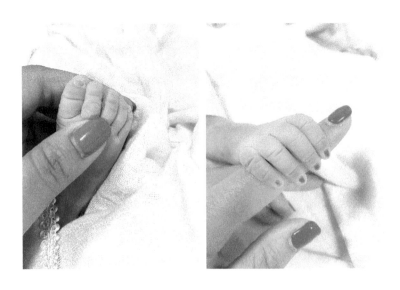

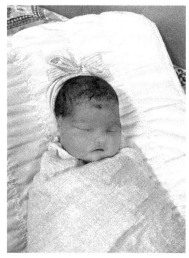
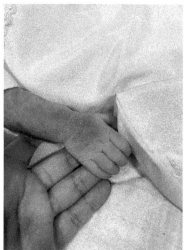

On my way out, I spoke to the funeral director about coming back the next day (Friday). He indicated they were booked solid with three funerals on Friday and that he couldn't promise that I would be able to come back to see her but that he would try to see if there was a gap during the day and would call me if it were possible.

I was massively disappointed that there was a strong possibility I wouldn't see her on Friday. But I didn't think it would be appropriate for me to make a fuss about it because the funeral director had literally gifted me more time with Eliana all week.

Leaving the funeral home that day, I had mixed emotions. I felt better because I was able to get rid of some of my regrets that had been haunting me and for that, I was truly grateful. However, I was sad because I wasn't sure if I would be able to see her on Friday which would leave me with only an hour with her to say goodbye before the funeral on Saturday.

Uhhh... the feeling of dread leading up to the funeral and my final goodbye on Saturday continued to hang over me like a dark heavy cloud.

Chapter 13

On Friday morning, I had called several times to see if it were possible for me to go see Eliana. However, at around 11:30 AM, the funeral home called to let me know it was not possible to accommodate my request today as they were using the gurney to do the make up for the funerals that day.

Although I knew there was a significant chance of this happening, I was still very disappointed. This disappointment cascaded into the anxiety and dread of my final goodbye tomorrow. Time was running out and now I had even less time with her than I expected or my heart was willing to accept. There was an overwhelming amount of anxiety over not knowing how I would survive without her little body which had provided me with such comfort since leaving the hospital.

That night, I didn't get much sleep, thinking about the dread of the next day. I prayed for God to give me the strength and for her funeral to be the most beautiful send off. If there was anything I could do for her here on earth, it would be that.

We woke up and hustled to get ready for the funeral. I was anxious to get to the funeral home and as usual, we were behind. As previously agreed with the funeral director, I had wanted to be there at 8:30 AM to review her dress and ensure her neck scars were not showing. However, getting everyone ready and out the door on time presented the usual challenge.

We finally got to the funeral home at 9 AM and I anxiously headed in. We were ushered to the small room upstairs for Eliana's viewing. It was not a fancy room but had a lot of windows and overlooked the grand entrance and staircase of the funeral home.

As we walked in, I quickly noticed the little white casket at the front of the room. It was the smallest casket I had ever seen, and it was holding our baby girl. What a reality to live! Though there were not many choices of caskets, I was pleased with the one we chose.

I laid eyes on her for the first time in the dress which I painstakingly spent hours trying to find, purchase and repurchase. The funeral team did a great job dressing her and were able to position the dress to hide her wound. She looked beautiful. Not wanting to spend a minute away from her, I pulled up a chair to sit with her, holding her little hand the entire time we were there.

Natalie and Alexander came and stood with her and I took a couple pictures of my 3 babies together. I wanted to document and remember Eliana's brief time physically here on earth. Natalie was still fascinated with her nose and kept saying how it was still quite bouncy as she poked it. Alexander came and played with her fingers, saying they weren't that cold. Eventually, I stopped Natalie from poking her nose as a bit of bloody liquid started to come out. I wiped it away softly with a tissue, like I would have for any of the other kids.

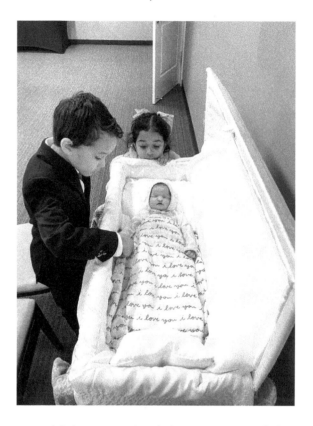

As I sat with her, I noticed the anxiety and dread I had been feeling the day and night before had left me; those feelings now were replaced with a calm and peace which could only be attributed to my answered prayers for strength.

Sitting and being close to Eliana's body had a calming effect on me and seeing the deterioration of her little body, I knew it was time for me to let go of her physical person. I was so grateful for the extra week we had together to transition to this point. Though we gave up ushering her body into the crematorium, the extra time that week by waiting until Saturday seemed critical to my readiness that morning to let her body go.

Slowly, our close friends and family started to arrive. I did not want to be rude and not greet everyone as they entered but I couldn't leave her side. They all came to pay their respects while I sat with her, and I greeted them as they came to view her body and express their condolences.

My friend Christin, who is the mother of Natalie's best friend Emer, came to pay her respects and handed me cards Natalie and Emer made for Eliana some weeks before she was born. The cards were a beautiful display of the love and anticipation that awaited Eliana and it seemed fitting they would be with her in her casket.

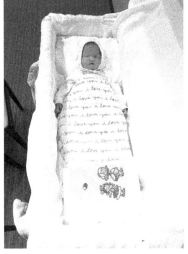

After leaving the funeral home on Thursday, I went to Target to see if I found a better swaddle blanket than the ones I found in BuyBuy Baby as I was still not content with what I purchased. As I walked up to the blanket section, I found "the one", a beautiful white muslin blanket with white writing saying "I love you" all over.

As time drew near to leave the funeral home, I asked if we could have ten minutes alone with her to say our goodbyes before they closed her casket to take her to the church. I draped the I Love You blanket over her body to tuck her in to her casket. I then placed the hand drawn cards by the girls in there, too.

I told her how much we loved her and that it was time for us to let her body go and for her to take her place in Heaven with Jesus and that I had to stay here with Alexander, Natalie and Dada until it was my turn to come be with her.

The funeral manager came in to indicate it was time to go. Ross and the kids said their final goodbyes and I kissed her hand, touched her forehead and let them close the casket.

As we headed over to the church, I continued to feel an unexplainable peace and strength. The church was beautifully decorated with white flower arrangements and framed black and white photos of Eliana. It was perfect and I felt pleased with the outcome of the choices.

We sat in the front pew and awaited the arrival of Eliana. We had decided not to proceed inside with the casket but stand as she was wheeled in by the funeral manager. The music, singing, and Father Jack's Homily were beautiful.

Most notable, Father Jack recited the below poem by Edgar Guest in his homily which was truly fitting for the occasion.

Like any parent, I never wanted to ever have to plan my child's funeral but as that was not a reality I could have avoided, I was happy with the beautiful sendoff we arranged for our sweet baby girl, Eliana.

After greeting and thanking the family and friends that attended Eliana's funeral, Ross and I followed the hearse to the crematorium as I requested. We pulled up to the back entrance and they got her casket out of the car. We took a few moments and said our final goodbyes with the casket closed as agreed previously. The funeral manager expressed his condolences to us for our loss and said he would be praying for our family. He said in his many years of doing funerals, these rare cases where parents bury their children are the hardest to be part of. We thanked him for his kindness and for their help with all the preparations and returned to the car. We watched from the car as they rolled her into the crematorium and switched custody of her body to the staff there.

To this day, the peace and strength I felt that day could only be attributed to the Grace of God. My prayers for comfort and strength were surely answered that day and Eliana's funeral and send-off could not have been any more perfect.

Chapter 14

For most of my life, I have approached the supernatural and associated gifts of veiled sight or prophetic dreams with a healthy dose of skepticism. Yes, I believed there were people that could see angels, good or evil spirits or that had dreams about future events perhaps but did not know someone personally who had any of these "gifts". This was until I was pregnant with Alexander.

In our family, it has been well known for some time amongst the cousins that my cousin "Geoffrey" dreams of babies coming into the family. I vaguely recalled when I was three months pregnant with Alexander that he told me the baby's name was Alexander and I told him that was impossible because our list had names that were only five letters or less due to Charbonné being such a long last name. Twenty-seven and a half hours of labor later and two-hour post birth without a name, Ross and I decided to call our baby boy Alexander after Alexander the Great, due to his strength displayed during labor.

On May 21, 2020, I found myself quite sad on what would have been my deceased best friend Natalie's 37th birthday, though she had passed away nine years prior and I had not cried on her birthday in several years. As I shed tears in the car, no one knew I was feeling extra sad on that day and I didn't mention it to anyone.

Candace and Natalie on July 24, 2010 at Candace and Ross' Wedding.
Photo Credit Jtography Story-Telling

The next day, I messaged Geoffrey over whats app messenger to ask if he had any baby dreams as we had been unsuccessful in the past few months of trying to get pregnant. He indicated he did have a dream, but it wasn't clear and that it was not unlike the prior baby dreams. After discussing the details of that dream, he asked, "How were the kids yesterday?" I replied, "They were ok. Why?"

He then said a certain someone was trying to say hi and that I needed to be happier on her birthday.

Knowing he was referring to Natalie, I said, "Aww, she said that. It sounds like her."

He said, "Yup, she (Natalie - my deceased best friend) was playing with them yesterday, or at least with them yesterday."

I smiled and replied, "Natalie (my daughter) said she knew it was Aunty Natalie's birthday."

After some back and forth, I said, "Ok, so next year, I'll throw Natalie a party with a cake! Is she in Heaven?"

He replied, "Very much so, but spends a lot of time with her family and watching over the children."

I asked if he was referring to Natalie's brother's children and he said all the children, especially her brother's kids, mine, and our other cousin's daughter.

For the years Natalie was sick and prior to her dying, she always told me that when she died, she would still be with me and come visit and that our friendship would go into Casper mode. The thought of this gave me comfort over the years and especially in the days and months and years after her death.

However, as years passed and the connection to her became noticeably infrequent, I became skeptical of my own experiences and feelings at the time, eventually attributing them to grief and just missing her. Sensing this in that moment, I think Natalie decided to prove her point through Geoffrey.

Geoffrey said, "Right now, she sent me an image of a bowl of rice for some reason and is just being really happy. I think it's rice... lol. Does that make sense?"

Surprised, I replied, "I'm making rice downstairs in a rice cooker!" How could she know that unless it was true that her spirit was visiting my house. Geoffrey also seemed equally confused as to what the bowl of rice meant as well as he was in another state and we were texting back and forth while I was upstairs and the rice downstairs.

It was incredible! For years, I had longed for a way to confirm my instincts about Natalie's spirit being with me but I couldn't see. Now Geoffrey was my eyes confirming what my spirit already knew.

After we got home from the hospital, Geoffrey messaged to check in on me and give his condolences. Needing to confirm she was okay, I asked him if he saw Eliana. He said yes that she was with Natalie and our grandfather and there was a big Angel kneeling down over her little spirit protecting her. This gave me great comfort.

Sometime after Eliana's funeral, I asked Geoffrey if he saw anything at the funeral. He explained that he saw a light with a unique color around me since Eliana died and that when he came to the funeral, the same unique color of the light around me was coming from the big candle on the altar. I asked him if he was sure the light around the big candle was the same light he saw around me and he said yes the big one the funeral guy moved a little when placing the flowers on the altar. I then explained to him the big candle was the Lenten candle and it was a big deal candle, symbolizing the light of Christ. I was in awe of the significance of this. The light and love of God was surrounding me and providing comfort and grace in my time of need. It explained so much of my feelings of peace and God's grace; that light surrounding me was the light of God; Jesus was with me providing much needed comfort. This conversation confirmed what I knew in my spirit to be true, and the revelation of the truth left me once again feeling so deeply loved and cared for by God amid such deep darkness and sorrow.

He then said that there was also a big angel on the altar which was the same angel he saw with Eliana's spirit before. The angel intently focused on Ross, the kids and I and he believed the angel was specially connected to our family and Eliana.

Lastly, he said that he saw a little girl with long curly dark hair skip in behind the coffin and skip back out with the coffin. In my heart, I knew that was Eliana and was at the time confused why she was presenting as three or four years old and not the baby in the casket. However, the reasons for this were revealed later in the journey.

Also, this was the first of many sightings of Eliana over the last couple years by others or myself.

Chapter 15

On Holy Thursday 2021 at 11:11 PM, while escaping to the mountains of Colorado, I reflected on Good Friday and specifically, the passion and death of Jesus. As I reflected, I was reminded of a profound conversation I had with the kids a few weeks earlier.

It was the Thursday after Eliana's funeral, and we were once again in the car on the way to school.

The day before, Alexander had been struggling with the loss of his baby sister and I was finding it very hard to find the right words to say to him. So, it was quite timely this conversation happened the next morning after I prayed for help.

The day started out like any other. We practiced Alexander's spelling words for the week in preparation for his test on Friday and then after, we listened to the song Oceans by Hillsong.

It should be noted that we've listened to this song every school drop off day for almost 2 years as a means of meditation on the way to school so much so that Natalie calls it "her" song and sings it for us every morning.

As the song started and the first verse and chorus below played, I drew the kids' attention to the words which resonated with me in that moment.

Oceans by Hillsong United
Songwriters: Joel Houston / Matt Crocker / Salomon Lighthelm

You call me out upon the waters
The great unknown Where feet may fail And there I find
You in the mystery In oceans deep
My faith will stand
And I will call upon Your name And keep my eyes above the
waves When oceans rise My soul will rest in Your embrace
For I am Yours You are mine[2]

I lowered the volume a bit and said to the kids, "The words of this song are very fitting for what we are going through with the loss of Eliana. It's saying when we feel very sad and we need help to get through the sadness, we can call upon Jesus for help. That grief and sadness can sometimes feel like water rising around us and like we are drowning but if we keep our focus on Jesus and pray, He will help us make it through. Also, sometimes we are called to step out in faith and just have to have trust in God's plan."

They seemed to understand what I was trying to say.

Then, out of nowhere, Natalie said after seeing a squirrel run up a tree, "Easter is about Jesus dying on the cross first and the Easter bunny second."

Alexander then quickly jumped in to correct her by saying, "No, Easter is the celebration the resurrection of Jesus three days after He died on the cross."

I confirmed Alexander was right about Easter being about the resurrection but it's also important to understand

[2] "Oceans by Hillsong UNITED. Sourced Musixmatch. https://g.co/kgs/bNXc2E

how Jesus carrying the cross connected to our everyday lives with our big and small hardships. I said, for example, Eliana dying is our family's own version of a cross we must carry, especially Mummy and Daddy. It may not be a physical cross like what Jesus carried, but it is something very hard and sad we have to go through, just like Jesus.

So just like the song says, we can pray for help and God will send the Holy Spirit or people to help us.

Natalie then said, "Yes, Mummy, like the friend that helped Jesus carry the cross."

Whoa, okay! Well, now I was totally impressed that at five years old, she made that connection and I credited this entirely to their wonderful Catholic School.

I said, "Yes, exactly like Simon of Cyrene who helped Jesus carry the cross, God has sent friends to help us carry our cross since Eliana died.

Natalie then said while showing me her biceps, "Mummy, I am very strong, I can help you carry your cross just like Simon helped Jesus."

I replied, "Peanut, you and Alexander do help me carry my cross by giving me hugs and lots of love and smiles when I am feeling sad about Eliana and even by having conversations like this."

After I dropped both kids off, I sat in the car for a moment, reflecting on the conversation and in total awe of what just happened. As I sat reflecting, the song Lead Me to the Cross by Francesca Battistelli came on my Christian streaming station and I knew that conversation was no mere coincidence. The chorus further resonated with me in that moment.

Lead me to the Cross by Francesca Battistelli
Songwriters: Brooke Ligertwood

(Chorus)
Everything I once held dear I count it all as loss Lead me to the cross where Your love poured out Bring me to my knees, Lord, I lay me down Rid me of myself, I belong to You Oh, lead me Lead me to the cross[3]

That day after school drop off, I had a long drive to run an all-day errand about 1.5 hours away from home. As I drove, I continued to listen to music and continued to reflect on the entire journey to that point.

I thought to myself: God never promised me an easy life and it is unrealistic for me to expect one when my soul is here to learn lessons and serve God's purpose. I believe the same is true for Eliana, even in her very short life. Jesus as the Son of God clearly didn't have an easy life when He could have had one but gave His life in service to God the Father's purpose and calling. Even if you look at the Saints, most, if not all of them, did not have a life without struggle.

Similarly, when Eliana died, I didn't know why this was God's plan and just needed to have faith just as Jesus needed to have faith in His Father's plan. It was not until God decided to share the "why and how" with Jesus that this happened. This is explained in one of several of the mediation scripts of the 1st Luminous Mystery of the Rosary, which is when Jesus was baptized by John the Baptist in the river Jordan and the Holy Spirit descended upon Him. At that point, the

---

[3] Lead me to the cross lyrics by Francesca Battistelli. Sourced Musixmatch https://g.co/kgs/mzi4am

mission he was to carry out was clear and God shared the Why and How.

Another song that played while I was driving that morning which resonated with me was "I Surrender" by Hillsong (note: I had never heard it or Lead Me to the Cross before). Specifically, the chorus below resonated with me as I felt throughout this whole season to that point I had surrendered to trusting in God and His purpose for Eliana and me.

I Surrender by Hillsong Worship
Songwriters: Matthew Philip Crocker

(Chorus)
Like a rushing wind Jesus breathe within
Lord have Your way Lord have
Your way in me Like a mighty storm
Stir within my soul
Lord have Your way Lord have Your way in me[4]

During this drive, I also reflected on Mary as the mother of Jesus. Father Jack pointed out previously that when the Angel Gabriel approached Mary to say she would become pregnant with Jesus, she must have been terrified amongst other feelings of being unwed during those times. Still, she said, "Lord, your will be done." Also, as Jesus' mother, it must have been excruciatingly hard for Mary to see Jesus carry the cross, beaten, crowned with thorns, and crucified. It is for that reason I know she knows what it was like for me to lose Eliana and what it takes to have unwavering faith in God's plan.

---

[4] "I Surrender lyrics by Hillsong Worship. Sourced Musixmatch. https://g. co/kgs/3kBsJh

As explained in a previous chapter, I began to pray to God for guidance as to whether we were to have a third child. I had prayed a lot about it alone without telling anyone, including Ross, about it. A couple days after I began to pray, my cousin messaged me out of the blue saying, "Are you thinking of having another baby?" This random coincidence was the sign I was looking for.

I recalled being so sure Eliana was going to be a boy, so much so that when we found out she was a girl, we had no name in mind. The kids liked the name Emma and tried to convince us to call her Emma Kate. In trying to honor their contribution to naming the baby, I began to look for girl names starting with the letter E. I remember coming across the name Eliana and liked it but never looked it up. For two weeks, the name Eliana stuck with me until eventually I looked it up.

Eliana's name means - God has answered.

In that moment, I knew that was her name and now I know that was the name God meant for her.

As I reflect on the journey of her short life, I believe that through her story, God is answering every person impacted in a personal and unique way through whatever part of the story that resonates with them. As a result, Eliana is serving God's purpose for her which was to impact others through her death. I personally believe people who die for the Glory of God and fulfill His purpose have a special place in Heaven. I am honored as her mother for her to have that special place in Heaven and would never begrudge her it.

Candace, Ross, Alexander and Natalie in Breckenridge Colorado
April 1, 2021. Photo Credit Shaili Stockham

Chapter 16

Since Eliana's passing, we have continued to treat her as an important living part of our family because, simply put, she is, living in the sense that her spirit lives on as she has entered her eternal life and thus remains connected to our spirits as part of our family.

If you think about it, during Mass every week, the priest says, "Peace be with you" and the congregation replies, "and with your spirit" Our spirits are part of our being, and it could be argued, the most important part of it.

I truly believe her spirit lives on and that she resides in Heaven in a very special place.

For me, one of the hardest parts of mourning a baby has been the absence of monthly milestones. Unlike Alexander and Natalie, Eliana had no developmental milestones; each month was just a reminder of the time that passed without her.

This was very apparent as I was part of a COVID baby boom in my circle of family and friends. There were babies who were born close to the time Eliana was whose milestones I was able to see though social media or family chats. There was actually one baby who looked very much like Eliana. Despite my grief and missing Eliana terribly, I made a conscious decision to not look at those mothers and babies with jealously or with a *why me* mentality. I recalled a conversation with my cousins, three of whom were due to have babies soon after Eliana passed. In our family, there is always such jubilation when a new cousin is born, and I wanted them to not feel like they had to hold back that joy because Eliana had died. I knew they wanted to be sensitive to our very fresh grief, but I assured them that I would rejoice with them once their babies arrived safely. I wouldn't wish what we were going through on anyone, far less my family. I actually mentioned to one of my cousins that if I were honest, out of the four of us, it is best it happened to me as I felt most prepared faith-wise for this not to completely destroy our lives and faith.

When I collected Eliana's ashes the week after her funeral, I spent days shopping for things to decorate her special place in our walk-in closet. I had wanted her ashes in our room close to us but also in a safe place out of the reach of the kids to prevent any mishaps. This also made it very easy for me to greet·her in the morning, during the day and at night. To this day, I still do it as it's one of the ways I connect with her.

At first, I thought to myself that I lost my mind, talking to her ashes but then reminded myself if I believe our spirits live on and have an eternal life, then talking to her and connecting with her spirit is more than acceptable and logical.

So anyway, here's where I say, believe it or not...

One Sunday, about two months after Eliana had passed away, I was changing the batteries in the LED candles in her special place in my closet. While changing the coin-like battery in one of the tealights, the battery fell out of my hand.

Rewind to about a year prior. I had read an article which asserted how dangerous these batteries are if swallowed, so although I was confident neither Alexander nor Natalie would ever put one in their mouths, I was still very concerned and didn't want to leave it on the floor. I spent ten minutes looking all over for it. I shook the clothes on the hangers, looked all over the floor and the closet on my hands and knees at one point and could not find it. I even shook the robe I was wearing, thinking maybe it was in a pocket or sleeve.

For obvious and practical reasons, I am in my closet daily to get ready in the morning and night and in general, in and out throughout the day as I mostly work from home and pop in to see Eliana at will from my home office down the hall.

Since losing the battery, I had been in there many times, constantly keeping my eye out for the battery. It has been two days with still no sign of the battery. Strangely enough, when it "fell", I remember thinking to myself that I never even heard it hit the floor which was strange to me. But I just said to myself that there was no other explanation. I also remembered saying when I couldn't find it, "Eliana, you should help Mummy find the battery as we don't want anyone to swallow it."

It was a Wednesday morning, 72 hours after the battery was missing when I walked into the closet and saw the battery perfectly laying on the floor in the middle of the walk path, complete with a little piece of the paper from the carton underneath it. The minute I walked into the closet, I saw it.

How could this be? I had been there several times over 72 hours and I can assure you, it was not there. Also, I did not mention to anyone it had fallen or it was missing, other than Eliana.

Ross does not go to my side of the closet and Lisa (my aunt) had not been in there since the previous Friday.

Additionally, if either of them found it, they wouldn't have left it on the floor.

Upon finding the battery, I picked it up and smiled and said thank you to Eliana and just marveled at what had happened and the sign she was clearly sending to me.

Mama, I'm here, just like you feel it and know I am.

After dropping Alexander to school this same morning, I went to Target to get some new soccer cleats for him.

On my way out, I stopped in the baby section and thought I'd get Eliana a little stuffy as a thank you for helping me find the battery.

I looked at several areas in the section and the stuffies available. Eventually, a single little stuffed cat caught my eye. As I walked over to the shelf, I noticed it was right next to the blanket Eliana was covered with in her coffin and I knew that was the one for her. Note that when I purchased the blanket for the funeral, it was on another wall.

When I got home and put it in her special place, it fit perfectly. I cannot ever adequately explain how this warmed my heart and gave me great comfort that her little spirit is with us.

Chapter 17

After Eliana's passing, I was experiencing a range of emotions with respect to her and her death. As time went on, I continued to notice and feel her absence. To be honest, Ross and I as well as the kids acknowledged almost daily how life is so different without her.

It was less than three months after Eliana died and I was due to return to work. The thought of going back to work full time, even though I was working remotely, still caused me great anxiety and dread.

I dreaded my first interactions with friends and colleagues.

I dreaded going into a meeting with someone who knew I was pregnant but didn't know she had died and being asked how's the baby.

I dreaded not being as sharp mentally as I was before she died because of all the trauma of the experience.

I dreaded my creative spark never returning because I was still so sad and grieving; my creativity stemming from my happy place.

There was so much dread, so much anxiety.

Six weeks after returning to work, I reflected on the experience of re-entering a familiar work setting as a different and forever-changing person. Overall, it wasn't as bad in some ways as I thought it would be, but it was also more emotionally exhausting than I expected.

First, I found that finding space to hold others' emotions with respect to Eliana's passing has been hard and exhausting.

Also, it did happen that a couple of people who did know I was pregnant but didn't know she died, I had to tell personally when they asked how the baby was. It was really sad for them to hear and for me to deliver the news.

There had also been a few people with whom I wanted to share all we've been through, but there was so much to explain. I was grateful to just direct them to the blog I wrote about the experience.

There were also a few meetings with awkward starts where people who were seeing me for the first time were not sure what to say or even if they should say something. The accompanying awkward silence was just that– awkward.

I also recall there were a few meetings where I was greeted with tears, condolences and touching check-ins.

All in all, though it had been emotionally exhausting, I felt the overwhelming love and support of my colleagues and friends at work and for that, I was and am forever grateful and consider myself blessed.

When I first started back working, my brain seemed spotty; it's hard to explain. Prior to Eliana dying, I was very switched on mentally, my work calendar was always synced with my head, all tasks were also synced as well as the kids and all their activities all in my head. Post Eliana, I needed to write everything down in many places and make reminders which would result in my still forgetting. As time went on, it got better, and I gave myself space and grace to get there, understanding my brain along with my heart and body had been through a major trauma, needing to be switched on in other ways to survive.

Overall, it took about three weeks for things to stabilize and for the heavy overwhelming dread to leave me as I completed the initial meeting rounds on the work circuit. At that point, the dread wasn't entirely gone but I was able to get back some semblance of my work groove which has always brought joy into my life.

At that time, I found the energy I had before was not as high and so I reserved and stockpiled it to help myself and Ross and the kids. There were still many things which didn't take from my "cup" before that drained me emotionally in those days. And yet, time was moving forward, and I was reminded about that constantly.

There were simple things like spring and allergy season ending and no more flowers on the trees. Other reminders like the end of the school year, Natalie graduating PK4 or even the opening of the Education Grant application period at work; there were just so many constant reminders.

When I went to the OB for the first time, pregnant with Eliana, the doctor commented that there was a massive baby boom. She was not joking. During COVID, there were so many people in my circle of family and friends that were also expecting. Since Elaina's passing, I prayed extra for all their safe arrivals. About four months after Eliana passed away, most of the expected babies were born. I had felt each time like I was holding my breath but was able to breathe easier with the news of a happy healthy baby and mama. I now imagine this is what it was like for all my family members and friends who in light of our loss of Eliana were also feeling similar sentiments at the time.

At this point in my journey, I was inundated on social media and in person with all the growing babies around me with their little milestones. This compounded my grief as I was unable to know or even imagine what Eliana would have been like at almost four months old.

As I learned to navigate life living without Eliana, I learned different things. That month, my biggest lesson and learning curve was Triggers. Unlike social media, there is no trigger warning for real life.

In the weeks following Eliana's passing while at school pick up, my head would be buried in my phone, trying to avoid eye contact or too much conversation with other parents who would genuinely ask how I was doing.

Around the four-month mark, though, I had been talking more and more to other parents at pick up and as a result, noticed a lot more around me. One day, as I stood up chatting with other parents and not in my usual spot, I noticed a mother with her infant car seat stroller. I recognized her as one of the other moms who was pregnant while I was pregnant. Noticing her stroller with her infant car seat attached broke my heart as I reconciled my reality that my stroller, car seat and baby were missing. That moment, without warning, emotionally unhinged me. I was so grateful that it happened on a Friday as it had given me the weekend to try to regroup.

Unfortunately, what I did not expect was that I would notice the mom and her baby almost every school pick up after that, for the remainder of the school year. This became almost two weeks of what felt like torture at the time. And in my face, it was a reminder that I couldn't avoid and believe me, I tried to avoid.

I've learned that month the hard lesson that these types of in-your-face reality checks are not as forgiving or as avoidable like the social media ones where I can choose to see the babies or just keep on scrolling.

A friend who knew my pain well said from her experience, she could be having the best day and out of nowhere, she would be triggered in the most unexpected way. This has been so true. My triggers were coming from the most unexpected places. That month was full of triggers.

Later that afternoon, we went to mass and the homily spoke to my heart and my pain. This did make me feel better but in the long run, the pain and cross still had to be carried and endured.

Chapter 18

Summer break was upon us with no more school pick ups until September, thank God! Towards the end of the school year, I had found out from Alexander that the kid whose mom and baby sister I was pained to see at pick up was moving to another school. I felt guilty for breathing a sigh of relief.

Little did I know that God had other plans.

In August, a few weeks before school opened in September, Alexander was invited to a birthday party. I decided to take him while Ross stayed home with Natalie. Soon after we arrived, I sat down in the shade on the patio, with a lot on my mind. While looking at the kids playing, I noticed Alexander's classmate and his mom walking in. "Oh no," I thought but then breathed a sigh of relief when I noticed the baby was not with them. It was not a huge party so there would really be no way to avoid us talking. I felt an immediate awkwardness about the situation. We had never spoken before, but we had an unspoken connection being "pregnancy buddies" at school pick up for several months and knowing how it ended for both of us.

At that point, I put on my big girl pants and embraced the situation, thinking there must be a reason we were crossing paths that day. We ended up addressing the elephant in the room and the connection we had. She was so gracious and kind that day, wanting to reach out before but like many, not knowing what to say. I ended up explaining all that had transpired with Eliana, and we truly connected on a deep spiritual level; we maintain that connection and friendship today. That day, the pain of seeing her and her daughter dissipated and was replaced with a smile for my new friend. This ended up being a really good thing as I found out that day, she had another son starting Kindergarten in September with Natalie. Thank God for His mercies, as He turned my pain into joy that day by connecting us. Seeing her baby girl no longer caused me pain but brought me joy.

Another thing I navigated that summer was how I wanted to respond to questions from strangers regarding my children. One Sunday, the kids had their first eye tests and as a result, we had to select frames for their glasses. The lady who helped us was very nice. She genuinely was paying me a compliment on how wonderful my kids were when she said to me, "They are such great kids. You should consider having a third child." I was totally and unexpectedly taken back by the compliment. I knew the sweet lady meant no ill intent and there is no way she could have known what we had been through less than four months before.

I found myself in that split second contemplating how to respond.

Part of me wanted to politely laugh it off and move on as she was a stranger and would be none the wiser. The other part of me felt that by not telling the truth, I would be denying Eliana, her existence and place in our family. After what seemed like a long pause, I said to her, "We actually did have a third child; her name is Eliana, and she passed away. This is her picture. She was beautiful and looked just like Alexander with Natalie's eyebrows [there I said it]." Without missing a beat, the kind woman said, "I'm very sorry for your loss. I hope you are doing ok."

I replied, "Given the circumstances, we're doing as well as can be expected."

There was no right or wrong way to answer that stranger's question but for me, I needed to speak the truth and not deny Eliana's existence as it would have weighed on my heart and caused me to feel guilty.

Chapter 19

I wouldn't be surprised if people reading about my journey can't fathom or understand how or why I was able to purposefully make the decision to turn to God through such a devastating loss. Honestly, it surprises me too sometimes.

Prior to having kids but after my best friend Natalie died, I had told Ross once that the grief and heartbreak I felt losing my best friend in the whole world (my person) was so painful and devastating that if we were to ever lose a child, I would probably have to be put in a padded cell because I would totally lose it. Fast forward almost nine years later and the unthinkable happened. The good news is I haven't been committed yet, though I'm sure many might think I've lost a screw or two or more, and that's ok.

In those days, as I shared my story, I constantly reminded myself that nothing I do is to please anyone but the ONE for whom my life's purpose is to serve and glorify. May all glory and honor be given to God in all that I do.

One of the main reasons I turned to God for comfort in the wake of Eliana's death was because the unimaginable pain that ensued was so overwhelming and immense that my heart and spirit knew it was only God who could comfort me. This is why it was important for me in the days after her passing to openly ask for everyone to lift us up in prayer to help me to fully step into that place and choice because truly doing that was not easy.

Though I wrote a lot and shared my thoughts and feelings on social media, in my blog and now in this book concerning my journey with respect to Eliana, I often feel no one in this world including Ross can fully understand the journey I am on and how I am feeling. Reflecting on this, it makes perfect sense if you look at it from the perspective that even two parents grieving the same child have their own unique journey of grief.

In my specific case, many times, especially in the beginning of grieving Eliana, I had feelings that were dichotomous in nature which were hard for me to explain and also hard for people to receive and understand. However, I believe this explains why choosing to seek comfort from God made so much sense. It's important to mention here that to me, God is not someone I made up in my head over the years to make me feel better. He is not someone I was brainwashed into knowing by a religious order, cult or my parents as a child. God is also not some scary, far removed, hard to reach being. My relationship with God is close, genuine and very real. It is also two-way and conversationally based in a divine love because God is love.

With God, there was no need for me to explain anything as He was there with me for every detail and moment before Eliana was conceived, for every moment before she died and for every moment after they said her heart stopped beating. He knows every thought, every feeling, every tear shed, every single detail, even beyond my own understanding as well as details seen and unseen to me. Sharing this intimate journey of grief with a loving and merciful God who continues to show me so much grace and love has been one of the most surreal and spiritually uplifting times of my life. This seems unbelievable as it's rooted in the most unreal and devastatingly painful experience of my life.

When I needed help, He sent the right person into my path to help me; when I needed to know He was with me and understood the deep pain of my broken heart, He showed me in a very real way that He was there for me. He turned my tears of despair into awe, wonder and humility. Over the first nine months of my grief, and even to date, God continues to show up for me and has left me thinking not only does He know my name, He knows what I am feeling and going through and He deeply cares for my well-being and loves me enough to be with me through it while comforting me like a best friend and in some cases, like a loving parent. It is for this reason I say I experienced a dichotomy of emotions.

At that time, the joy and peace I felt being close to God who was with me and within me every moment of every day was so life giving that I could only imagine and hope to one day experience this fully in Heaven.

Randy Kay's book, *Revelations from Heaven,* spoke so much truth about the things I had been experiencing in the first nine months of my grieving, things I found hard to put into words or explain. Reading his book has affirmed so much in my mind, despite my heart and spirit not needing the same affirmation.

My major take aways from Randy's book was that God wants a relationship with us, one where He holds our hand, guides and comforts us as we travel through the mountains and valleys of this life while fulfilling and finding our God-given purpose.

Also, at that time, the song "Scars" had been coming on alot. It highlighted another dichotomy I lived. The song truly resonated so deeply with me because I can see Eliana's death and everything that has happened to us as a family since, being used as a story for the Glory of God and having brought about so many positive changes. For weeks, I had wanted to write a blog expressing this sentiment. However, I hesitated to include it because part of me felt a lot of guilt for saying I wouldn't change what happened to her. Truth be told it took a lot of time for me to work through those feelings and gain a greater understanding and perspective. Eventually, I let go of that guilt because it served no purpose as it was not my choice whether my beautiful daughter lived or died, nor could I change the reality. The only thing I was in control of was how I interacted with God in the wake of her death. And that was and remains a choice I have ZERO regrets about. Choosing to walk this painful path with Jesus by my side and, in some cases with Jesus carrying me, saved my life and spirit. By sharing this deeply personal and painful journey with Him our relationship deepened significantly. His light and love rescued me from the darkness of my grief, leading to a greater and deeper understanding of my purpose and Eliana's purpose, as well as allowed me to tap into a joy and strength that could only come from the Lord.

Ephesians 1:11: *In him we were also chosen, having been predestined according to the plan of him who works out everything in conformity with the purpose of his will.*

Chapter 20

Following Eliana's death, some of the hardest things I have done have been out of my deep love for others. After all we had been through with Eliana's death, family and friends were very understanding in situations where I chose to not do something I did not feel I was ready to do. In all situations, I weighed the cost benefit for my heart and my Spirit at the time. If the conclusion didn't serve my heart, my healing or God's purpose, I opted out.

One such instance was meeting my niece Penelope. The last four weeks of my cousin-in-law's pregnancy with Penny were filled with complications, non-stress tests and overall worry for Penny and Ashley by all those who loved and supported them. I prayed a lot during this time for Penny and Ashley's safety as well as remained on high alert and standby to care for the boys, in case she came early.

Penelope was born exactly eight months to the day after Eliana, on 18 October 2021. Prior to Eliana dying, the unspoken plan had always been for Eliana and Penny to grow up together as the last two baby cousins in our two families.

Though we have a large family, we have few family members in the area and only one with little kids. My cousin Joe is my mom's sister's son and although we grew up in different countries, me in Trinidad and Tobago and Joe in Oklahoma USA, we reconnected as adults when they moved to the area around the time Alexander was born.

Joe's kids are the only cousins our kids have living close by, so the bond they have is special and treasured.

Many times over the years, when we had decided to do low key birthdays, it's always been cake and playdates with cousins. So, when Rex Joe's second child's third birthday came just two weeks postpartum for Ashley, we were on cousin duty to ensure "brother" (as we call him) had a birthday party. Prior to Ashley giving birth, this was the plan as we knew things would need to be low key while she would still be recovering. I also knew that this would be the first time we would meet Penny, but this was a detail I tried not to focus on.

During the months after Eliana left us, I recognized the importance of setting expectations and boundaries during my grief, to ensure my healing is done according to my own pace. As Ashley and I ironed out the plans for Rex's birthday, I expressed that there was a strong possibility that when I met Penny, I may not be ready to hold her. I did my best to assure Ashley it wouldn't be for a lack of love for Penny but because my heart may not be ready to hold another new-born just yet.

Weeks before meeting Penny, I experienced an unex-pected trigger at another birthday party from which my heart took days to recover. We had attended the birthday party of Natalie's best friend Emer. At the party, as I had expected, her baby cousin Madison was in attendance. Madison's mom and I were due a mere day apart in March, so Madison being born at the beginning of March meant she and Eliana were born just two weeks apart. I had seen Madison before briefly with no issue, so I didn't expect to be triggered.

At the party, I focused on other people and things and didn't focus my attention on the baby. However, as the party wound down, the adults sat at the dining room table chatting. Chris, Emer's mom, had taken Madison from her mom while she helped her brother. While sitting on Chris' lap, Madison started to grab for the slice of birthday cake in front of her. Without missing a beat, Chris proceeded to give Madison her first bite of frosting ever. Madison was delighted and kept opening her mouth for more as she quickly finished it. Her reactions and desire for more frosting were so cute and everyone at the table, including me, were now totally focused on Madison. Madison and Eliana were practically the same age and I couldn't help thinking what Eliana would be doing: would she be the same size as Madison or smaller; would she be also wanting a taste of the frosting as well as going from hand to hand around the table like Madison. Amid all these thoughts, I then notice Madison who was now with our friend Lak holding Ross' baby finger.

In that moment, my heart hurt seeing Ross with her little fingers wrapped around his pinky. We went home shortly after this, and it took days for this unexpected trigger to wear off.

With this recent experience so fresh in my memory, I started to become anxious about meeting Penny. Honestly, for almost the first year since Eliana died and even some instances after, I always experienced a lot of anxiety leading up to dates and events I knew would be hard for me emotionally. However, with the effects of this recent trigger still fresh, my anxiety was compounded.

The day of Rex's party arrived, and I could feel the heaviness around me emotionally. I played awful tennis that morning and didn't understand why until I was on my way home. I ensured Ross was handling soccer and the kids so I would have time to go to Eucharistic Adoration as I knew I needed to go pray over it and ask God for strength.

Prior to leaving for adoration, I went into Eliana's nursery to gift baby Penny a few things from her cousin Eliana. This was hard as I had not gone through the still perfectly organized drawers in months. It is important to know at the time there are only two babies who were gifted items of Eliana's; Esme Eliana's womb best buddy, predetermined best friend and daughter of my dear friend Molly, and Penny, her cousin. This was not easy. Going through Eliana's unused things and remembering every moment I purchased or received each item with such joy and anticipation just hurt. When I left for adoration, I had already felt the impact and residual sadness from the previous exercise.

As I entered the chapel and I knelt down in front of the Blessed Sacrament to greet my Lord, I felt like a child who had had a bad day at school and who was holding back all my emotions and tears all day until I was in the arms of my parents. It was in this moment I was overcome with a wave of emotion, understanding, love and compassion. It was as if Jesus was saying, "I know exactly what you are feeling and I'm right here with you, feeling your pain deeply with you." I immediately started to tear up because I felt what was on my heart was being seen and heard by God and I was not alone.

Before I started to pray, I wrote in my prayer book my intention to have strength and comfort to get through the day. Halfway through saying the Rosary (which I listen to with headphones on my phone), I noticed time seemed to be going slower than usual. Each Hail Mary was longer and more pronounced. I would have found this strange if it weren't for the recent podcast I listened to about a Near Death Experience (NDE) account where the author asserted that God has the ability to slow time so that those who are dying have the opportunity to do what they need to do in their final moments to get to Heaven. This obviously wasn't a near death experience for me, but it was a time when I didn't want time to rush on and it didn't.

After the Rosary was done, I went to my playlist to hit shuffle. As you know, hitting shuffle on my playlist and letting Jesus be the DJ was, and to date is, one of the ways God talks to me. I hit shuffle on my 42-song playlist and without fail, God showed up for me. The first song was Rescue by Lauren Daigle (there was a 1 in 42 chance that song played). As you may recall from a previous chapter, that was the song that Jesus played in my car for me as I was totally broken after shopping for a blanket for Eliana in her casket for the funeral. It was the song that has played for me in my lowest moments, so for it to be the first song to play on this particular day was a miracle and Grace from God. It should be noted that in the four months prior to this, I had not heard Rescue more than three times. Tears continued to stream down my face as the song played because of the big feelings I was feeling but also because I just felt so understood and held by God who was suffering with me, like a friend supporting a friend during something hard.

(I encourage you at this point to listen to each song in order to really walk with me through this story).

The next song was Surrounded by Michael W. Smith which also spoke to me and the fact that I see myself fighting my battles and hard moments on my knees praying like I was that day.

The next song to play was Blessings by Laura Story. This song also had major significance as it was the song that incessantly kept playing through a major conversation I was having with Jesus back in August when I questioned why it was necessary for Him to give me a gift, only to take it away.

At this point, I decided to stay for five songs instead of my usual three because the DJ was good. We were taking pizza to Pennsylvania and I had set the time to pick up the pizza at 1:15 PM which meant I needed to leave adoration at 1 PM. God, in His infinite wisdom, knew this and would you believe, the last song finished playing at 1 PM. Literally, in perfect timing.

As I knelt one last time before I left, I offered up my suffering of that day and all my suffering in this life due to Eliana's passing for the intentions for others written in my prayer book because, according to Saint Padre Pio, no suffering should go to waste so I offer it up!

I left adoration feeling marginally better which was strange, as usually when God gives me so many messages, I feel so uplifted and it's enough. But that day was different.

Previously, I had heard the story of Saint Maria Goretti who had offered up her suffering on her death bed for the salvation of sinners. This offering by Maria remained on my heart as I continued to pray for so many weeks. Then one day in adoration, about 6-7 weeks prior, I said, "Lord, I offer up my suffering in this life without Eliana for all the intentions for others written in my prayer book, especially those who are sick." I am not sure if I knew what I signed up for in that moment but since I started to do that, it was as if the buffer between me and my suffering was partially removed and the pain I felt was now somehow more painful. It's hard to explain, but I chalk it up to thinking if I offer up my suffering, I need to feel the pain for it to be a worthwhile sacrifice. The upside of this was that many I've been praying for believe my prayers have worked or are working for them.

As I left adoration to pick up the pizza, I was still not feeling wonderful and not sure what to do. At 1:11 PM, I was inspired by the Holy Spirit to call Molly, so I did just that. There have been very few people I have able to connect with in respect to Eliana that were able to just be with me and meet me where I was at any given moment. That said, it was safe to say Molly was a Godsend for me, essentially one of His promised soldiers sent to help me. We went through every day of our pregnancies together and she continued to be a light in my life as I fulfil my purpose and role as a mother of a child in heaven.

That day, Molly and I spoke and cried together for a while as I expressed my pain. The Holy Spirit was right to tell me to call her because I felt better after we talked.

While Molly and I were still on the phone in the car, and I was now parked at home, Natalie came to the car to greet me and asked, "Mummy, why are you crying?" I replied, "Because of Eliana. Today is just a hard day for me." Natalie then said in the sweetest voice, "It's ok, Mummy. Eliana is in Heaven but you have me. I'm here with you and going to give you a big huggees to make it all better." Natalie continues to be such a blessing in my life with her beautiful spirit, and her huggees did make me feel better (a little soldier in God's army).

As we drove to Pennsylvania, Ross, and I spoke about how I was feeling. We acknowledged it was hard but that we needed to do it as Joe and Ashley and the kids were there for us when Eliana died. They were by our side during Eliana's funeral and were part of the select few that saw her when the casket was open, which I am sure was not easy for them. We chalked it up to this was what family does for family and we are going to show up for them, Rex and Penny.

The kids were so excited to go see their cousins and to meet their baby cousin Penny. However, Alexander did say he was also feeling a bit sad as he also wanted to be able to hold Eliana but never got to. Natalie was bursting with excitement at the seams.

As we got there, I felt I was in as good a place as any, given the situation. One of the wonderful things about my cousin Joe and his wife has always been things are just really easy and laid back with them and us, so I just went with the flow.

As the kids greeted each other, it felt like any other cousins meet and greet. Joy, excitement and fun filled the air.

Honestly, the details escape me with the exception of a few key moments. The 1st moment was when Natalie held Penny for the first time. What a bittersweet moment. She was beyond excited, yet so gentle and loving. The moment, however, was cut short so there was not much time to dwell on it as Rex saw Natalie holding Penny and got territorial and then insisted to hold her which made Ashley and I laugh.

Then Alexander came over to hold her and he was as awkward as I had expected him to be. Poor Penny at this point was now screaming for someone over the age of seven to hold her.

The moment that eventually got me was, however, when Penny went to sleep and Natalie wanted to hold her again. Ashley put Penny back in her arms on the chair and they were just perfect there together. Natalie even said at one point, "I'm such a good big sister to Penny." That comment gave both Ashley and me a slight punch in the gut moment. As I stayed there supervising Natalie with Penny, I had a moment alone with them. In this moment, I honored my feelings of sadness never able to see Natalie hold Eliana. The sadness that the conversations we had about Eliana being cold to the touch and frozen was totally different to the conversations about Penny being so cute and needing to keep warm. Such a stark contrast eight months later! Ross came over to see Natalie with Penny and also teared up with me. It was painful to see how good she was with Penny. It was painful to watch them and mourn the life we didn't get to have with Eliana here on earth. Natalie would have been the perfect little assistant and big sister. It was not lost on me that Natalie will always be a big sister to Eliana just as I will always be her mother, but the experience of her living life in Heaven makes the experience here on earth different.

Eventually, after Natalie's arms got tired, Penny continued to sleep in her MamaRoo baby swing. I passed by a few times just to check on her and touched her little fingers which were warm compared to Eliana's. I realized I felt no rush for me to hold her and that it had been such an emotional day for me, there was no need to push myself more than I had to. I was also released of any pressure to hold her as Ashley honored me by not putting me on the spot to ask me to hold her; I appreciated that more than she would ever know. This allowed me to take my time and honor my heart through the experience.

As we sang happy birthday to Rexie and saw the joy the cousins had being together that day and also how much it meant to Joe and Ashley we were there for Brother, I knew it was worth the effort and pain.

I wasn't ready to hold Penny that day but left feeling like the 1st time was over and that the next time would be easier.

Natalie and cousin Penelope

Chapter 21

The minute we hit January 18, 2022, exactly one month before Eliana's 1st birthday, I started to feel the underlying heaviness of the unknown. What were those days the 17th and 18th of February going to be like for me? How were we going to celebrate? *Were* we going to celebrate? Would I be in the mood to celebrate? Would I tailspin into sadness with this unreal milestone? So many unknowns loomed over me. The reality that we were approaching living one entire year without her with us was pretty unbelievable. How did so much time pass?

What made things worse was that my birthday and Alexander's birthday were before Eliana's. Added to this was the reality that my birthday kicked off birthday season in our household. Other than Christmas, Birthday Season has always been our favorite time of year as we celebrate all our birthdays within six weeks. This has always been something very special to us as a family.

Birthday Season starting with me and ending with Ross with all the kids in between:

- *1 February - Me*
- *8 February - Alexander*
- *18 February - Eliana*
- *1 March - Natalie*
- *16 March - Ross*

Given all that was on my mind, I managed to keep it together for most of January as we headed into my birthday – that is until a few days before my actual birthday. The kids, with their excitement for birthday season, reminded me every chance they got that my birthday was coming and birthday season was upon us. Also, as the day approached, Ross and some of our friends started to ask what I wanted to do for my birthday. I was honest and said I really did not want to celebrate but eventually agreed to dinner with just one other couple which ended up being a nice lowkey no fuss celebration.

On the evening before my birthday, things felt like they were on the brink of falling apart. Knowing that the only person that could help me was Jesus, I went to eucharistic adoration and found myself in tears, just praying for the strength to get through the next day. I felt so heavy.

One of the lovely things about birthdays are all the calls you receive from friends and family. However, I didn't feel up to talking to anyone. The idea of having to pretend to be good or happy seemed like a lot of effort, so I let my family know I would only take messages on the day but not phone calls.

On the morning of my birthday, I thought about my 30th birthday and I realized it was very similar to my 40th. Natalie, my best friend in the whole world, died three months before my 30th birthday and I was still feeling a massive weight of grief due to her loss. The party I planned to have never happened and my sadness and grief was propelled by the fact that for the 1st time in over ten+ years, Natalie wasn't the first birthday call I received. That reality didn't make for a great 30th birthday.

I then set my sights on my 40th to have the birthday celebration I didn't have at age thirty and up until Eliana died, that was the plan. Being the planner that I was, I had already started to look for venues and entertainment for the big bash.

Overall, birthdays in general tend to make one reflective; however, milestone birthdays even more so.

That year, Birthday season for me personally was not the exciting or joyous time it would usually be because of the reality that we were approaching Eliana's 1st birthday in Heaven. A reality that was never expected when I dreamt of this 40th birthday and that was so unbelievably sad.

With my emotions raw, I decided to take the day off from work to focus on regaining my emotional balance. That morning, I spent two and a half hours in Eucharistic Adoration, praying and listening to my Jesus playlist randomly with the Holy Spirit as my DJ.

After praying the Rosary, I hit shuffle and was in awe by the fact that in each moment every song that played spoke to my feelings as they progressed. It was as if I were having a conversation with God in real time and the songs were answering and comforting my heart and spirit in each moment. God was so faithful that day, truly being with me through the lowest of lows and lifting me up to a stable and peace filled spirit.

I did not take any calls that day except for one. My mom called and called several times, making me think it was an emergency. So I answered. She was very worried about me and felt bad I didn't want to take any calls. So, when I answered on Facetime and looked like my normal self, she was surprised.

After adoration and the call with my mom, I spent some time shopping for new decorations for Eliana's space in our home. Doing this has always helped me feel better as it's one of the few things for her here on earth and it was needed that day to help me fill my cup so I could embrace the fuss my two children on earth wanted to make on my birthday later that day.

I ended that day with the following reflection: My 30's started out with a year of grief and ended with a year of grief but in between, there were also so many blessings to be grateful for.

The week of Eliana's birthday, I decided it was necessary for me to take the entire week off work to pray, prepare and grieve as needed. I had had such a grace-filled experience on my birthday, praying and being with the Lord, I knew that was exactly what I needed to do while preparing for her birthday. Each morning that week, I went to mass, then to eucharistic adoration for a few hours and in the afternoon, I spent my time making decorations for her birthday celebration. I eventually decided that we would celebrate her birthday together at home like we did for Alexander and Natalie.

On the 17th, which was the one-year anniversary of her dying in my stomach, Ross and I spent the day together to honor that day. I recalled us going to mass that morning. On the drive to the church after school drop off, I was telling Ross how important it was that he slowed down and find quiet time to be in prayer with the Lord. I explained it was in the quiet with God that we can focus on what He is telling us and what He wants us to do. We were listening to Jonathan Cahn's *Book of Mysteries* audibly before this comment. When the book resumed just after, we were taken back that the next mystery he spoke about addressed this very sentiment.

I laughed and said to Ross, "You see, it's not just me saying find the quiet; it's God. This mystery was for you."

In the homily at mass, Father Dan had espoused a similar sentiment which made me smile at Ross. We then proceeded to go to lunch together. On the drive, the audio book kept speaking to our conversations as if God was weighing in on the discussion. It was remarkable, to say the least. These things I had become accustomed to, but it was the first time it was happening with another person present and based on our conversation. Prior to these coincidental messages where the Lord weighed in were affirmations of thoughts in my head where I needed guidance or support. Many times, when I would experience these godly affirmations, guidance or support, I would share them with Ross, but part of me always thought that though he would never say it, he was skeptical believing it was my mind just seeing what I wanted to see.

Before we got out of the car, I mentioned something new that had started to happen to me a couple months prior. I explained I had wanted God to speak with me more directly than through music. In actuality, I had prayed to hear the voice of God and that I believe my prayers had been answered when one day in adoration, I was led by the Holy Spirit to google a number combination on my phone. When I did it, the Bible verse spoke to exactly what was on my heart and what I was praying over. Since that day, it continued to happen again and again. When I mentioned this to Ross after it first happened, I noticed a slight skepticism from him that it was indeed happening but being the good husband he was, he never once said he didn't believe it was happening.

In the restaurant, we talked about Eliana and many of the things we experienced that day one year prior, both individually and together. We also discussed some current events related to Ross, specifically at work. At some point in the conversation, I said to Ross, "If you open your heart and pray for God to lead you with the Bible verses, He will." And just like that, with a leap of faith, I said to Ross, "Let's see right now if the Lord has something to say to you." I looked at my phone and showed him the random number combination and then googled Bible verse number:number which was my usual practice. As I read the verse that came up, I was shocked; it worked! The verse spoke exactly to the conversation we were having just minutes before like a third person in the conversation putting in their two cents. Ross was amazed but also skeptical, thinking it was a fluke. I returned to my phone a few minutes later as our conversation continued and saw another random number combination which I googled in the same way: Bible verse number:number. WHOA! Again, this Bible verse added to the conversation, this time affirming it was no fluke. Our conversation continued and I did it again almost 10 minutes after the first instance and it happened again! three times in 10 minutes. I myself was taken back by the miracle we witnessed together. I said to Ross that this is truly amazing because there are 30,120 verses in the Bible so that there was a 0.0003% chance any one of those verses would come. He was totally blown away. I then said, "Well, now you are plugged in to the Word of God in this way from my experience, it is important when you ask for the guidance that you follow through on the advice which may not always be what you want to hear but it is what you need to do." Ross left lunch that day, forever changed.

The next day was Eliana's 1st birthday; it was pretty surreal that an entire year had gone past. Most of it seemed like a blur and then again, it also seemed so in focused. I decided to keep the kids home from school so we could spend the day together, celebrating their sister.

We went to mass as a family, which was really special. Specifically, the Gospel of Matthew that day spoke to me. Mark 8:34-35 says that Jesus summoned the crowd with His disciples and said to them, "Whoever wishes to come after me must deny himself, take up his cross and follow me. For whoever wishes to save his life will lose it, but whoever loses his life for my sake and that of the Gospel will save it." When Eliana died, a part of me died with her. That day, just one year and one day before, I was invited (though it didn't seem like an invitation at the time) to accept my cross and return one of my babies to Heaven. The past year had been a testament to me picking up my cross and following Jesus and the reading was spot on with how I was feeling on that day.

After mass, we went to Eucharistic Adoration, prayed the Rosary as a family, and picked up lunch at one of our favorite restaurants. Earlier in the week, I had emailed Father Dan to see when he would be able to come over to bless the house. One of the earliest days that worked for us was the 18th. I took it as a sign that there was no better day to bless the house and Eliana's special place in our home than on her birthday. So, I invited Father Dan over to bless our home and have lunch with us. This turned out to be the perfect celebration for us so much so that time had got away from us and Father Dan had to leave before we had cake.

In retrospect, this worked out perfectly as I had a moment to be in my emotions about the day. We had the now looming ceremonial cutting of the birthday cake. I realized I had not decided whether we were going to actually sing happy birthday or just cut and eat the cake but then I remembered Natalie's message through Geoffrey almost two years prior about celebrating her birthday. It should then be no different for Eliana and we should celebrate her birthday which would include cutting the cake.

We gathered around the beautiful cake and birthday décor. I lit the candle and told the kids they could blow the candle out together for their sister. One thing I adore about Alexander and Natalie is their love for singing Happy Birthday and boy, they did not disappoint. With lights dimmed and in the loudest most beautiful voices, they sang happy birthday to their sister in Heaven while I recorded it with my phone.

After I served the kids some highly anticipated birthday cake, I reviewed the video I recorded. To my surprise, I noticed right away a little flutter of light bouncing around the kids and cake as they sang. This was the most jovial little light, which was a beautiful sign from Eliana that not only was she there with us but she loved the celebration we had for her. This was all I wanted, for her to feel the tremendous amount of love we had for her in Heaven. It was the perfect message from Heaven from our beautiful baby girl, a message very much needed and very well received.

I ended the day by posting the below Happy Birthday dedication post to Eliana on Facebook.

God's #truth is our #truth Over the past year, we have chosen as a family to controlling the only thing we have control over - Our Faith and our immense love for our baby girl.

We had a beautiful celebration for Eliana on her birthday with Mass and Eucharistic Adoration as a family followed by lunch and a wonderful blessing of our home with Fr. Dan.

Eliana's life over the past year has impacted us as a family in a truly wonderful way, given the circumstances. The lessons in faith, hope and trust are lessons each of us will have forever and will continue to grow and nurture.

As time has progressed on my journey in particular, I have come to truly accept and agree with God's big picture of His plan for my life and the life of our baby girl and for this, I am eternally grateful because the resolve and peace that comes with this is beyond comprehension or my ability to adequately explain. All I can say is a life full of God's purpose and meaningful impact is what we were put here on this earth for and the fulfilment from this is enough to sustain our existence and leave you wanting for nothing but God. Each of us is born with a God-given purpose; however, it is our duty and essentially our choice whether we accept this purpose and subsequently seek out God, the truth and our purpose.

In my entire 40 years of life, I have never had a closer or more real two-way relationship with God and for that, I am grateful to Eliana and her impact on me in this regard. I am also tremendously humbled by God for the continued clarity on my purpose, for His companionship and guidance daily, for His comfort in all my times of need and for wisdom and discernment for the truth according to Him. I am also beyond grateful for all of the above and for His dedication to securing my salvation, for demonstrating unconditional love and for His ultimate sacrifice for my sins.

Eliana continues to impact so many lives in so many miraculous ways and I am sure in ways I will never know or fully understand until it is revealed to me in Heaven.

We are only here on earth for a short period of time; at best, we get 100 years which, when divided by infinity, is just a drop in the bucket. In so many of the books I have read over the *past year including the Bible there is a theme of focusing on our heavenly lives versus life here on earth so as not to be caught up in the pain, struggles, noise and chaos or even the good things.*

My mama bear instincts know where my littlest cub is and nothing will stop me from spending my eternity with her when my sweet Lord and Savior calls me home.

Until then, I continue to love her and mother her from earth while she resides in Heaven and continue to give thanks for all this journey has to offer.

Curious what the energy was like around us on her birthday! This pretty much sums it up! This is the joy that is rooted in the love of God. There is also an unexplainable little light fluttering around which I only saw after I saw the video. I guess she liked the celebration.

Chapter 22

Have you ever heard the saying God works in mysterious ways?

I, for one, have always been fascinated with the mysteries of God most prevalent in the Bible but also woven throughout my life and the lives of others. Simple things like your path crossing with someone where the person impacts your current situation and life in a positive; or perhaps being in the right place at the right time to help someone in need; maybe there is a random billboard or bumper sticker that speaks to what is on your heart as you drive by; or perhaps something bad happens to you and it redirects your path in life.

With respect to the mysteries in the Bible, this fascination and learning has been fed by books such as Jonathan Cahn's *The Book of Mysteries* which contains 365 mysteries from the Bible which are explained.

More specifically, the mysteries of God's work in my life are found through a retrospective lens, where upon reflection, I can see how I am being strengthened or redirected on my path for my own betterment, even and especially in cases of the hard things.

Below is a testament to how intentional God has been in my life which in the grand scheme of the world seems so insignificant, yet the intentional nature of God makes me feel so loved, treasured and special.

After Eliana died, there was a period where we (Ross and I) bounced between the mindset to try again or totally shelf the idea and just move forward. It is safe to say for a while, we were not in agreement on the way forward. I was in camp try again and Ross was in the camp no thank you, I never want to even chance going through what we just went through again.

I had started to go to Eucharist Adoration (henceforth referred to as Adoration) around the end of June 2021 and had committed myself to going once per week. This, at the time, spiritually seemed like a natural next step in my faith, to continue to strengthen it on my journey with God. Little did I know God planned to magnify and speed up this process ten-fold. Prior to February 2022, I attributed the reason for the trial endured as God getting me to go to Adoration six days a week to pray for others. Although I had accepted His purpose, I boldly questioned why all the additional pain was necessary and as a result, I fundamentally disagreed with the method used by Him at the time. In my shortsightedness, I simply thought, if God wanted me in Adoration six days a week, He could have just asked and like every other time in recent past I would have complied. However, it was only after February 2022 in hindsight I was able to identify it was also a tool to strengthen me for a future path I was to walk.

Anyways, at the end of July 2021, we found out I was pregnant. This news was met with a tremendous amount of joy. This joy, however, was short lived as it was totally derailed by a not-so-great 1st doctor's appointment with the Obstetrician (OB). When I went to the OB at six weeks, they were unable to find a heartbeat. This being my first ultrasound since the ultrasound that confirmed Eliana had no heartbeat was a literal punch in the gut to once again have to hear, "We don't see a heartbeat."

The doctor indicated that given I was just six weeks, it wasn't uncommon, and we probably just checked too early. He would do blood tests and we would see what happens. The consecutive blood test results and ultrasound had given conflicting messages and I was quickly unravelling with the roller-coaster of emotions and a lack of clarity of what was happening. I had never had a miscarriage before, so it was just foreign territory. The fear of the unknown was eating me alive.

Unable to focus and in a place where I felt my mental and emotional stability and faith was being rocked to its core, I decided to take the week off work to regain my balance. Even upset and confused as to why God would allow this to happen to me after all we had recently been through, I still turned to Him for answers. So off to Eucharistic Adoration I went. For hours daily, I just sat, cried, prayed and spoke to God.

My conversation with God on the Monday was very telling where I was emotionally.

I asked God, "Why you would give me this gift to take it away?

Why would you crush my heart like this?

I have done everything you have asked of me since Eliana died and you do this. You led me to believe there was hope!

What is the point of this cruelty? You misled me…"

Despite what had happened with Eliana, I never once had this type of conversation with God. I never asked why. But this time, I was just so hurt and confused and was being crushed by the weight of my anxiety and worse fears that I decided to put it all out there for the Lord.

My practice at the time was to say one Rosary and listen to three songs after hitting shuffle on my playlist. So, after voicing my disapproval of God's unconfirmed actions, I prayed the Rosary and hit shuffle on my Jesus playlist to see if I would get a response. The unfortunate thing for me in that moment was that I did get an immediate response; however, it was one I did not want to hear.

The song Blessings by Laura Story came on and my tears flowed as I listened to it. Below are some of the words that were the hardest to digest.

Blessings sung and written by Laura Story

What if Your healing comes through tears?
What if a thousand sleepless nights
Are what it takes to know You're near?
And what if trials of this life are Your mercies in disguise?[5]

After I left Adoration that day, the same song kept playing randomly in the car. It came on a total of three times as I drove around and each time, I changed it almost immediately, refusing to accept this was my answer. (Note: Before this, I hadn't heard that song for months and hadn't heard it more than a couple times ever).

The next day on Tuesday, I returned to adoration; I prayed the Rosary and prepared to hit shuffle. However, before I hit shuffle, I said to God, "I do not want to hear that song again because that (aka I'm losing this baby) is not what you are telling me!"

---

[5] Blessings by Laura Story. Lyrics sourced on LryricFind https://lyrics.lyr-icfind.com/

I hit shuffle and Blessings by Laura Stories came on again. In total defiance, I hit shuffle again and it came on again. So shocked that happened, I said, "OK, fine. It seems like I am not in control of this conversation... I am listening." Done arguing, I prayed for strength to make it through whatever the outcome according to God's will. Thy will be done.

The rest of the week, the songs were more along the lines of strengthening me and giving me peace. By the time my appointment on Friday came around, I was in a place of peace and spiritual strength. On my way to the doctor, I hit shuffle and the song *Another in the Fire* came on, further letting me know God was with me. By that time, I was pretty sure the news was going to be bad as I also started to spot that morning. I was diagnosed with a missed miscarriage and the doctor said that since I was now nine to ten weeks along without a natural miscarriage, we would wait the weekend to see what happened and then consider other options the following week.

That night, I woke up at approximately 4 AM, sneezed three times pretty hard and it was over. It had been five weeks of an emotional rollercoaster so to be spared the physical pain, I thanked God for small mercies.

After our miscarriage, Ross was even more sure he didn't want to try anymore. I remained on the fence as time went on. Eventually, in late December to early January, I said to God, "I am truly content with Alexander, Natalie and Eliana and don't want another child, but this is just my opinion. You know my life is YOURS so may Your will be done for Your Glory." And just like that, I left it there.

As February approached, the weight of our family's 6-week birthday season starting on February 1, loomed over me. This was going to be my 40th birthday and it was not shaping up in any way to be close to what I had imagined or planned. And then there was Eliana's first birthday on February 18 and all the unknowns of how I or anyone in the house would feel going into and on her birthday also loomed over me. There was also my indecision about what we would do and how and if we would celebrate her birthday.

> **Note to reader:** *Although I discussed in Chapter 21 events surrounding Eliana's first birthday this Chapter brings to light many details not shared about the same time period but relevant to another aspect of the journey that happened concurrently.*

For months prior, I had been asking God to speak to me in more direct ways, not through others or songs but directly. I had thought that when I started getting number combinations which led me to specific Bible verses, my prayers had already been answered. However, on the morning of February 14, my prayers were answered in the most unexpected way. That morning, in my dream (which was only audible), God said to me, "You are having a son and his name is Jeremiah." I had never had a dream remotely close to this when God had spoken to me. I woke almost immediately and responded to God while smiling, "Ha-ha, nice dream, ok, whatever." It seemed so impossible. We had tried for several months with no success and had also suffered a miscarriage. This month, in particular, was so emotionally charged we made a conscious effort to steer clear of any such activities. How could this be true or real? My period was due any day, so I quickly dismissed the dream and continued planning for Eliana's birthday later that week. The next day, February 15, I noticed an increased need to go to the bath-room and my mind started to replay the dream and what was said to me. I kept thinking to myself, "It's impossible!" We literally were avoiding anything that could result in this situation. Also, I kept thinking even if it is true, I don't know if I have the mental or emotional capacity to deal with this just three days before Eliana's birthday. I decided at that point whatever the situation was, I would wait until the day after her birthday to confirm if my period didn't come.

By 7 PM that night, I had gone to the bathroom more than seven times for the day. Not knowing was now becoming a distraction and I really just wanted to be fully focused on Eliana's birthday prep. I said to myself, "Just take the test. You don't care either way but at least you will know and can refocus." I proceeded to take the test and in under ten seconds, there was a bright second pink line. I could not believe it. I started to laugh and smiled and said to God, while looking upward, "I guess thank you. I hope you know what you are doing." I went immediately and showed Ross who was just as surprised as I was. I told him about my dream the night before and said God had told me yesterday and I didn't believe Him. I explained that God said to me in my dream "You are having a son and his name is Jeremiah," and as a result we didn't have a choice in his name.

None of our kids had ever been a surprise. I often joke and say we are just not surprise people. To be honest, I really don't like surprises and it's very hard to surprise me. This however was a total surprise, one that we welcomed whole-heartedly, a blessing we were beyond grateful to God for.

If you thought, whoa, that's totally unbelievable, there is more. So much to unpack...

Back in January, my cousin who is infamous in our family for dreaming babies coming, sent me a message on

WhatsApp from halfway across the world to ask me if I was pregnant. I said, "I definitely was not as I had my period, so it was definitely not me…"

So, after I found out I was indeed pregnant, I wrote my cousin still halfway across the world to say:

Me: "So, remember last month when you asked me if I were pregnant?"

Cousin: "Yeah."

Me: "Well, I am pregnant and the day before I found out, God told me in a dream, 'You are having a son and his name is Jeremiah.'"

Cousin: "You're kidding! Jeremiah was the baby's name I saw a while ago."

The name Jeremiah means "appointed by God".[6]

At twelve weeks, we confirmed via a 98% accurate blood test and an ultrasound that we were indeed as God said – expecting a son.

And if I thought that would be the last revelation and signs of this mystery, nope; it just kept going…

After Eliana died, I had a lot of time on my hands and decided to throw myself into a project to redesign our family picture wall to include Eliana. One day, while looking at the wall, I thought, "Ok, where would we put a picture of Jeremiah?" Most fittingly, his place would be under Eliana and between Natalie and Alexander. As I focused and zoned in on the Bible verse currently posted there, I was taken back when I realized it was Jeremiah 29:11.

Jeremiah 29:11: For I know the plans I have for you, declares the Lord, plans to prosper you and not to harm you, plans to give you hope and a future.

How intentional is God; my mind was blown! For over a year that Bible verse from the Prophet Jeremiah had hung there with only God knowing it would be replaced with a picture of Jeremiah, our son to come.

Another miraculous coincidence is that I would turn 37 weeks on 5 October. Since Eliana died at 37w 6d, I had always been told that any subsequent pregnancies wouldn't go past 37 weeks. October 5 is the feast day of Saint Maria Faustina. The connection here for me was Eucharistic Adoration. I go to Adoration six days a week; this has undoubtedly strengthened my faith even further to be able to walk this current path. Eucharistic Adoration is essentially praying in front of the Blessed Sacrament and according to her bio, Saint Faustina is known as Faustina of the Blessed Sacrament. What are the chances that out of 10,000 saints recognized by the Catholic Church I would hit 37 weeks on the Feast Day of Saint Maria Faustina?

The final thing I wanted to share, though honestly the list goes on, is while driving one day in the car, the song Promises by Maverick City came on and it occurred to me that just seven days before God told me about Jeremiah, I had the dream on February 7, where I was praising God, singing, "*Great is your faithfulness to me*" from 2 AM – 4 AM. This was a song and melody I had never heard before. I spent most of the morning trying to find the song, pretty sure it must have been buried in my playlist When I eventually found the song and heard it for the first time, these words resonated most with me. The song played like a story of God and me for the past year.

Promises by Maverick City Music
Songwriters: Aaron Moses/Dante Bowe/Joe L. Barnes/ Keila Marin/Lemuel Marin/Phillip Carrington Gaines

God of Abraham
You're the God of covenant
And of faithful promises
Time and time again
You have proven
You'll do just what You said

Though the storms may come and the winds may blow
I'll remain steadfast

Great is Your faithfulness to me
Great is Your faithfulness to me
From the rising sun to the setting same
I will praise Your name
Great is Your faithfulness to me [6]

However, that day in the car knowing this dream pre-ceded the dream about Jeremiah just seven days before, the

---

[6] Promises Lyrics by Maverick City Music. Sourced: LyricFind https://g. co/kgs/dUho5U

following words jumped out to me as being directly connected to the overall message from God which was, "I have
given you this Word and you need to trust and have faith in
Me that it will happen."

> *And let my heart learn, when You speak a word It will
> come to pass* [7]

A couple of nights ago, Ross and I sat outside under the
stars talking while listening to my Jesus playlist. Ross said
while we were in Punta Cana, he woke up one night and
couldn't go back to sleep. While up, he looked at me while
I slept and started to worry something was wrong with the
baby and he was in distress. This worry almost led him to
wake me up out of concern, but he decided not to.

I expressed I wasn't surprised this happened to him as he,
like me, went to bed the night before Eliana died knowing
she was alive and fine.

I said that the kids also have a level of anxiety about
the situation which is understandable. Natalie had said to
me while in the delivery room that she wanted Jeremiah to
stay here with us so bad and she hopes he doesn't die like
Eliana; Alexander had expressed a similar sentiment earlier
on in the pregnancy.

I said to Ross, "I am going to ask you the same thing
I asked Natalie. What did God tell me? 'You are having a
son and his name is Jeremiah.' What did God tell Alexander
in class as they stayed still to hear God in the quiet? 'The
baby will be fine.' So, what should we believe? The devil lies
but God doesn't lie. He is the truth. So it's either believe

---

[7] Promises Lyrics by Maverick City Music. Sourced: LyricFind https://g.
co/kgs/dUho5U

what God has told us and have faith or we live the next few months, driving ourselves crazy with worry and anxiety."

As I finished saying this, the song Promises came on the shuffled playlist. And I said, "You see, even God is saying we need to relax and trust that His Word will come to pass. Everything will be ok."

Being pregnant again just under one year after Eliana died and after a miscarriage less than six months prior, it would be normal and expected for me to have a lot of anxiety and be on edge. However, just the opposite occurred. I could finally see in hindsight the fire of the miscarriage trial I endured was meant to prepare me for my pregnancy with Jeremiah. As a result, I was having a peaceful and calm pregnancy because of God's grace and preparation; I intentionally chose to remain prayerful and close to him believing in His Word spoken to me.

I was having a son and his name is Jeremiah.

Jeremiah 1:5: Before I formed you in the womb I knew you. Before you were born I set you apart.

ELIANA

Photo Credit Kristen Nicotra of KArtocin Photography

Chapter 23

At my 26th week appointment, I took a routine one-hour glucose test to check if I was at risk for Gestational Diabetes (Note: I did the test earlier than 28 weeks because I was at high risk). I had done this test while pregnant with Alexander, Natalie and Eliana and had failed it every time but always passed the subsequent three-hour test. I even recalled telling the lab tech this as she did my blood draw. So, when I got the results, I had failed the one-hour test and needed to do the three-hour test, I was definitely not surprised or concerned.

The following week, I returned as expected to the doctor's office to do the three-hour glucose test. The worse part of the test, other than the horrible drink you need to consume, was the long period you need to fast. Fasting is usually not an issue for me, but it's very hard to do while pregnant. That said, after the three-hour test, I rushed home to eat and no surprise; I had a meeting as well soon after and didn't have time to eat. As the meeting started, I became very lightheaded and almost fainted while sitting down in my office chair. You know things are bad when you are in a virtual meeting and the other people in the meeting are asking, "Are you ok? You look like you are going to pass out." By the grace of God, I didn't pass out and was able to eat and lay down the rest of the day, but for a moment, it was pretty scary. However, even then, I didn't think much about it and just passed it off as fasting related.

My test results from the three-hour glucose test came within days of taking the test via my LabCorp account. One of the nice things about the LabCorp results is seeing the results of the last time you took the same test next to your new results for comparison. As I opened the results, I noted that this time, I failed three out of four blood tests which made me positive for gestational diabetes. This should have been the most alarming thing to me when I received the results; however, it wasn't.

It should be noted that in order to be positive for gestational diabetes, you need to fail two out of four blood tests.

My eyes were instantly drawn to the results of the test when I took it while carrying Eliana. It was the first time I ever saw it. I barely passed at that time, failing one of four. And then there it was. My Ah Ha moment. Could I have just barely passed my glucoses test because I was exercising and laid off the carbs the night before and then developed gestational diabetes soon after testing? Could stopping exercising and going into Christmas and Birthday season have propelled me into the condition? Is it possible to have had it and never even known? Everything in my gut said yes. I started to research gestational diabetes and outcomes and, low and behold, stillbirth was one of the prominent possibilities. Not only was it a possibility but one study stated if gestational diabetes goes untreated, there is a 45 percent increased risk of stillbirth. And just like that, I knew deep down this was what happened to our Eliana. I took the test on 24 December 2020 and barely passed. After this, all exercise stopped and sugar season started with Christmas and birthday seasons. With no controlled diet due to not knowing, her little body was trying to make insulin for the lack of insulin my body was making. She was very sick, and we never knew. The fact I had extra amniotic fluid also supported my hypothesis that this is what happened. But I was no doctor or expert, so I needed to ask my doctor if it was possible that I could have developed gestational diabetes after testing. I needed to ask if I could have had it and never knew…

At my next doctor's appointment, I asked just that. The answer was yes, it was possible but obviously at this point, there was no way to know for sure. However, this was all I needed to know because nothing about Eliana dying ever made sense up to this point. My rolling over onto my stomach in my sleep or sleeping on the wrong side just never made sense. And that there seemed to be no reason for her dying also never made sense. We had never done an autopsy, so it was never confirmed. There was nothing wrong with my placenta or blood tests. But this, supported by the excess fluid levels, made total sense. My mama gut knew this was it and it was revealed to me by God at a time when I was at peace with her death and able to accept the newfound information with seriousness and urgency to help save Jeremiah from the same fate.

My doctor immediately started me on a strict diet of low to no carb, no sugar diet to get my blood sugar under control. The first six days were brutal. I was pregnant and hangry (never a good combination). This adjustment in diet worked for the most part with the exception of my overnight fasting number which was never below 95 when I woke up. Because my fasting number wouldn't become regulated, my doctor put me on ten units of insulin to help.

When we got home after picking up the insulin at the pharmacy, I could see it on Ross' face. He wasn't up to the task of administering my injections, so I would need to self-administer in my side. Right love handle it is! I had never been so happy for a fat pocket on my side because the leaner areas just hurt more. We continued to monitor my morning fasting number for three days and it was decided by my doctor to incrementally increase the dose to twelve units. It was not an easy eight weeks and two days of injecting myself with insulin. There were so many nights I would touch my skin with the needle and have to find another spot because it was so sore. As my belly continued to grow, it was impossible to alternate sides as I needed to use my right hand to administer. But my big baby belly wouldn't allow me to reach over. My side was very sore, and as the weeks went on, it was harder to find a spot to stick the needle. But I knew what the outcome could be all too well and was not about to let anything happen to Jeremiah. So, I did what was necessary and offered up the pain and suffering to God for His Will to be done here on earth.

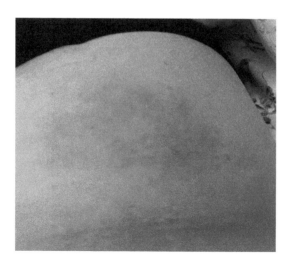

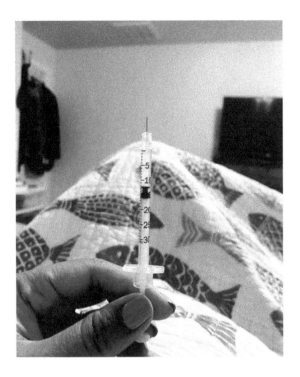

On top of the insulin, the whole restricted diet and testing my blood sugar six to eight times a day came with its own challenges. In the first two weeks, I had been really regimented with my diet. I was literally eating the same things over and over which was frustrating enough, but then things that hadn't been blowing my blood sugar started to blow it. This happened for three days and I was starting to lose my balance with the frustration. With no answers apparent, I started to pray for guidance. A little voice started to say, "It's not you; it's the blood sugar monitor. It's broken." It took me three days and a lot of prayers and frustration to finally listen to the voice and do a control test. The control test was totally off the mark and the voice was right, of course! A faulty machine was the cause of my additional stress; the devil was messing with me. The next morning, I purchased a new blood sugar monitor and regained my sanity.

Due to being high risk, I had a lot of doctor's appointments. One of the standards of care for pregnancies like mine required me to be seen by Maternal Fetal Medicine (high risk specialist).

At my 18-week appointment, I recalled the doctor diligently combing through my file saying that since there was no clear reason why my previous pregnancy ended in "fetal demise," she didn't see why I couldn't carry this baby to forty weeks. Eliana died at 37w 5d, so going to forty weeks sounds very difficult emotionally and mentally But I decided not to focus too much on it as we had a lot of time to go, and it was in God's hands when Jeremiah would come.

In my 20-week appointment which Ross attended with me, we were greeted by the most empathetic maternal fetal medicine doctor of the lot. Dr. E. entered and apologized for our loss of Eliana and then said," So here we are, the Baby after the Baby which, in many cases, is the hardest baby to carry." I could feel my eyes tearing a bit as he acknowledged this reality. He was right; it wasn't easy but I kept focusing on God's words to me, "You are having a son and his name is Jeremiah." I brought up to him my concern about what his colleague said to me two weeks before about going to forty weeks. He said he understood. He stated that there was no medical need to induce before but too often, the mental and emotional stress of the mother carrying another baby after such a loss is not taken into account. He said he didn't see the need to torture me to go past the age that Eliana was when she died, though he wouldn't say 37 weeks exactly. Sometime that week he would be ok with and that decision would be made with my OB closer to the time.

At my 26-week appointment, I saw another doctor. Alexander and Natalie had gone with me and everything with Jeremiah was fine so other than realizing Alexander was super smart in connecting that Sona technology used on submarine was the same used in ultrasound, it was quite uneventful.

One of the things I cherished most after Eliana's death was the 3D ultrasound picture a gracious tech gifted me two weeks before she died. I was 35 weeks pregnant at the time and because of my excess fluid, we were able to get three beautiful clear pictures of her. Even from inside the womb, she was gorgeous and my love for her grew that much more as I could imagine her little face with such accuracy. Knowing how much I treasured this keepsake, I decided to schedule a 3D/4D ultrasound for Jeremiah just two days before my 30-week ultrasound in the hospital. During the ultrasound, Jeremiah was hiding his face so we tried a lot of tactics to get him to cooperate, including jumping jacks, until we eventually got a great picture of him.

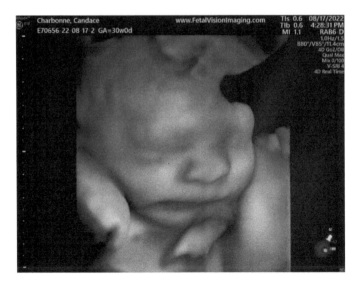

The next day, while I was getting a pedicure, I noticed that I did not feel Jeremiah move in a while. I started to worry that he got hurt the day before when we tried to get the right position to take the ultrasound picture. Instant fear and regret overtook me. A little voice inside kept saying, "He's OK; you are just overreacting. Once you are done here, just go home and lie down and you'll see he's fine." Ignoring the voice, I messaged Ross to say I was concerned about Jeremiah's movement and I was considering going to my doctor's office just to check on him. If that happened, he would need to pick up the kids at school. Ross, being his supportive self, told me to keep him posted. I told him I was going to give it a little longer and would let him know.

So distracted by this, I had forgotten to choose my color. The nail technician handed me the basket of nail color samples. When I went in that day, I had planned to get the beautiful pink color I had two weeks prior but changed course and selected a random blue because I thought it looked nice. After the color was put on my toenails, I was taken across to the manicure station. Still worried as he had not started to move yet, I was preparing to call the doctor and message Ross to pick up the kids. It felt like I hit 30 weeks and my nerves were unraveling and my anxiety through the roof. These last few weeks were going to be hard.

As the technician removed my nail polish, my eye caught the blue nail polish bottle with gold writing. I picked up the bottle with my free hand to read the name, "Walk on Water." Not believing my eyes, I blinked several times and read it again. WALK ON WATER. I then replied to the voice that was telling me earlier he was ok. Message received. I needed to calm down and keep my eyes on Jesus because these last few weeks would require such a deep level of trust for me to be able to do the impossible. Just like the apostle Peter walked on water, I would have to keep my eyes focused on Jesus. What an incredible message and reminder from my loving God who was telling me, "It's going to be hard but all you need to do is keep your eyes on Me and you will be able to walk on water."

Not long after this, Jeremiah started to move. I messaged Ross to let him know all was okay and showed him the picture of the bottle.

At my 30-week appointment, I saw the same friendly doctor I saw with the kids. After reviewing my scan, the doctor indicated that she didn't see why I couldn't go to 39 weeks with this pregnancy. There it was again. Another doctor saying I should go past the point Eliana died. I told her that I wanted it to be considered that they induced me sometime during the 37th week. She then firmly said there was no medical reason at this point to consider a 37-week delivery and that she didn't see why I couldn't go to 39 weeks. I then said to her, "You've read my file, right? You know I suffered a stillbirth at 37 weeks 5 days?" She said, "Yes, I know that but there is no statistical difference between a stillbirth happening at 37 week and 39 weeks."

I then said, more upset than before, "I get that but because I have had one, my personal statistic has gone up." I was very upset at this point and decided to save my peace and just end the discussion there. I then said, "my last growth scan is scheduled for 34 weeks, so we should have another scan after that to have a better idea of how big the baby was and so on to help make decisions."

She said, "yes, we can schedule another growth scan at 38 weeks." This hit a nerve. My voice of concern for Eliana had been minimized and I had felt I did not follow my gut and advocate for her enough when I had the chance. So, this nerve that the doctor hit was sensitive.

I said firmly, "Having another growth scan at 38 weeks means you will not be giving consideration to my request to inducing in the 37th week. Can we not have another scan at 36 weeks?"

She pushed back and said, "Growth scans one to two weeks apart show no real difference. At a minimum, we can put growth scans three weeks apart to be able to see a difference."

I replied, "Well, we should schedule the scan for 37 weeks, so due consideration could be given to my request." She agreed, though under protest.

This was the last time I saw this doctor as I requested only to see Dr. E for the rest of the pregnancy. This required me to follow him to all three of his office locations in the area. But I refused to be upset again. I was blessed; the kind woman at the front desk was able to personally empathize with my pain and thus was very accommodating in changing all remaining appointments (eleven in total). At the end of our call, she asked me if I wanted to put in a formal complaint against the doctor, but I said that I forgave her and wanted to just move on.

That day was the first day in the entire pregnancy I had become upset to the point of tears. I felt so unheard and treated like a statistic versus a person who lost a child and buried that child. I held myself back from asking the doctor whether she had ever delivered a dead baby and handed her to the mother because if she had, she wouldn't be speaking this way which was so insensitive to what I had been through. I had also held myself back from saying that in this state, I could walk into an abortion clinic at 37 week and say I didn't want the baby anymore due to mental health reasons and they would kill the baby (horrific idea which I am fully against), But I couldn't ask them to consider bringing him out early to save him because I was afraid he would die like his sister if he stayed in longer. The thought was so upsetting. A lot of prayers had to be said to keep my balance that week and ultimately forgive her insensitivity.

At my next appointment with my OB, I explained what happened at maternal fetal medicine with that doctor and was greeted with more compassion. The nurses explained that it was due to the insurance which made it hard for the doctors to induce before 39 weeks. My doctor empathized with me and said sometimes the doctors are inexperienced with these things and that doctor probably hadn't experienced a stillborn birth in her career. At this point at 32 weeks, we still had time; he assured me that he heard my concerns but we should wait to discuss further in a few more weeks but that at that point, he was aiming for 38 weeks.

I got in the car and thought to myself that 38 weeks was better than 39 or 40 but still not ideal. While driving, I said to God that everyone kept pushing this idea of 38 weeks and beyond. Is this what God is asking of me? To have faith in Him to go beyond 37 weeks and 5 days? I decided at this point to pray over this and await an answer from God to my question. I then switched to the most urgent need at that moment, food! I had to pick up my daughter Natalie from camp but needed to eat before that. I saw a Mc Donald's and decided chicken nuggets would meet my dietary restrictions and serve the purpose, though not the healthiest choice. As I placed my order in the drive through, my mind continued to reflect on the question, is God asking me to trust His word and for me to face my fears to go beyond 37 weeks and 5 days? As that thought was finished, I pulled up to the 1st window to pay and I handed the cashier my card. While looking at the cashier, I read his name tag. I couldn't believe it; his name tag read JEREMIAH. That was way too coincidental to not be intentional. In that moment, I knew the answer to my question posed to God was a resounding yes. I needed to trust God completely and carry Jeremiah past the time when Eliana died. This was the path I had to walk. This was what was being asked of me. Right then and there in my heart, I said, "Lord, if this is what you ask of me, this is what I will do. May Your Will be done."

Chapter 24

I decided to start my maternity leave at 34 weeks instead of 38 weeks like I did with Eliana to allow myself no distractions with work. I wanted to totally focus on what was happening with Jeremiah. Though I did not think Jeremiah would be making any early appearances, I regretted not being more focused on Eliana toward the end of my pregnancy with her. Also, with so many doctors' appointments, it made more sense just to be on Maternity leave. At this point, I had two appointments a week at maternal fetal medicine and one at my OB.

During my 34-week OB appointment, we discussed the results from my 34-week growth scan. In the scan, we had confirmed that Jeremiah's kidneys were still presenting with dilation, but this was not a major concern. Also determined in the scan was the fact that Jeremiah was estimated to be 7lbs which was up from 3lbs at his 30-week scan. Due to his rate of growth being significant and the fact that babies of mothers with gestational diabetes tend to be on the larger side, my doctor said to me, "I don't know about you, but I am ready to induce at 37 weeks and get this baby out. What do you think?"

Totally surprised by this, I smiled and said, "If this is what you think is best, then yes, let's book a date and get him out. 37 weeks is 5 October." He then looked at his calendar and said 7 October we would induce.

When I got back into the car, I breathed a sigh of relief with tear-filled eyes. For the first time, I could see the end in sight and I could start tentatively imagining holding Jeremiah on the outside. I took a moment to google the date October 7, to see if there was any feast day or significance to the date. My google search indicated that October 7, was the Feast Day of Our Lady of the Rosary. What a fitting date! The Rosary was a prayer that was so integral to my story and journey of faith to this point. It was the prayer that I said with my Rosary group at work that set me on the path to strengthen my faith to survive Eliana's death and strengthened my faith far beyond that point to where I was that day being 34 weeks pregnant with Jeremiah. I took this as another divine confirmation that everything was going to be fine, and I should continue to pray and trust in the Lord my God.

At my 35-week appointment, I started to request details for the induction with the OB Coordinator. She indicated that since the induction was going to be scheduled for October 7, I would need to call the hospital at 2:30 PM that day to ask what time to come to the hospital. Knowing the kids had school on Friday and trying to plan ahead, I asked if we could schedule the induction for the 6th so I could go to the hospital Thursday night instead of Friday night in hopes Jeremiah would come out and we would be able to bring him home on Sunday to meet the kids. As it was one day earlier, my doctor agreed and we scheduled my induction for the 6th, knowing nothing would likely happen until the 7th.

During my 36-week appointment at MFM, I requested to see the doctor as I wanted to ask a question. I had started not to sleep as well as I started to worry what side was best to sleep on. Though the entire pregnancy to this point was fairly free of anxiety given my history, I could tell as we got closer to induction I was starting to be more on edge. When I requested to see the doctor, I thought I would see Dr. E, however, another doctor walked in and here I was with a new doctor who was unfamiliar with my case for me to ask what now seemed like a silly question about which side to sleep on.

To my surprise, the doctor immediately acknowledged we were almost to the end of my pregnancy and that given what happened last time, I would likely not be sleeping much as we approached induction the following week. His kindness in acknowledging the unspoken anxiety of things to come put me at ease to ask my "silly" question.

I explained that Eliana had died while I slept and that I just wanted to confirm whether there was a better side I should be sleeping on. He indicated that either side was fine and I should avoid sleeping on my back for too long. At the end of our conversation, he asked what the name of the baby that passed away was. I told him her name was Eliana. He said he thought that was her name because he noticed my necklace and appreciated that I honored her by it. That day, I counted my blessings again for another empathetic doctor at MFM that really helped to calm my nerves.

As we inched closer to induction on October 6, I felt myself getting emotional. My final appointment with Dr. O was on October 5. I recalled going into the office, feeling very emotional. The nurse could tell I was emotional and asked if I was okay and I said, "Yes, it's just a lot." She replied, "Don't worry, you will have your baby in your arms soon. Dr. O is the best; everything will be ok." I just nodded quietly with tears in my eyes.

It was too much to explain at the time, but I was not worried that Jeremiah would be ok. This I knew in my heart would be the case based on God's promise. However, I was being taken back to Eliana's birth and the stark contrast I was about to experience with Jeremiah. The last time I had been induced and given birth, there was a deafening silence in the room with a baby that, though the most beautiful of my children, smelled like death. I was grateful we were not giving birth in the same hospital as this would have been a bit too much.

That night, I felt relieved that it would be my last night taking the insulin. This felt like a transitional step in our journey. Surprisingly, I slept fine that night and had a subdued mood heading into the day. Prior to this, a lot of friends and family who were aware of our induction date kept saying that I must be excited. When talking about it, Ross and I agreed that excited wasn't the word we would use to describe how we were feeling. We were, in fact, quite anxious to get it over with and have Jeremiah safely in our arms.

On the 6th, induction day, I did my required COVID test at the hospital and went for the highly debated 37-week growth scan. The last MFM doctor I saw had said though I would be induced the same day of the scan, he wanted to do the scan to allow my doctor to go into delivery with as much information as possible.

Per the instructions for induction provided by my OB's office, I called the hospital's Labor and Delivery at 2 PM to ask them when I should arrive for my induction. They indicated that there were no beds available and that they would add me to the list and call me once a bed was available.

I did not receive a call, so at 8 PM I called again to see what the situation was. They indicated that all rooms were still taken and to call back.

That night, I called back at 12 AM and again at 4 AM, only to get the same message despite explaining I was a high-risk induction. The nurse who answered understood the situation but explained women in active labor continued to arrive in the hospital and had to be given any room that became available. She further explained that they were so full that all their overflow rooms were also in use. I hardly slept that night, thinking I would miss the call for the bed, so I did the only thing that made sense to do–I prayed. This was super unexpected, and we were not sure how to proceed and decided to wait until 6 AM to call Dr. O's answering service; we didn't want to wake him up. Dr. O called me back soon after and explained he was actually in the hospital and there was truly no bed available; however, he would work on it and get back to me. He also indicated that if 11 AM came and there was no bed, I should still go to the office for a Non-Stress Test for the baby, just to double check all was ok. Within an hour of calling Dr. O, we got a call from the hospital saying to come in at 8 AM. The car had been packed since the night before so we just got ready quickly and shared an apple in the car as there was no time for breakfast or so we thought.

We finally arrived at the hospital but couldn't find a parking spot. It was pretty incredible. It was 8 AM on a Friday morning and there were several cars waiting to snag a spot. After about 15 mins of waiting, we finally got a spot. Though we had done this before, we continued to follow the instructions on the piece of paper from the doctor's office. Bullet three on the sheet said Please bring everything that *you need once you arrive as you will not be permitted to leave and come back. This includes car seat, toiletries, necessities and clothing for a few days.* We had everything but were surprised by the instructions to bring the car seat. Both Ross and I re-read the paper and confirmed it said including the car seat. This seemed strange to us as we didn't understand why Ross wouldn't be able to leave to go to the car and get the car seat. The hospital was still operating in COVID times, so we said ok, we guess we take the car seat with us. So, we popped the car seat onto the stroller base and headed inside, against our better judgment.

As we walked into the hospital, we commented on how much it would have sucked to walk out with an empty stroller when we left the hospital without Eliana and that by taking the stroller in now, we were setting ourselves up for this possibility should something go wrong. Once again, we reminded ourselves of God's promise and held on to it. Check-in at Labor and Delivery took over an hour as our room was not ready even though we were told by the lady on the phone to get there within the hour. Still pregnant and hungry, I began to regret not slowing down and allowing us to get some breakfast beyond the shared apple in the car and two nut bars.

The waiting area was not big and we were taking up quite a lot of space with our car seat and suitcase. The reception nurse said the stroller wasn't necessary at this point and that we didn't need to bring it but now we were tagged, we couldn't leave. Sigh. We knew we should not have brought it but told them it was on the paper from the office, so we just did what we were told. They said it was ok and there was enough space in our room for it.

When our room was finally ready, I heard a nurse say to another, "Eliana, your induction is here." Knowing how tired and emotionally charged I was I passed off what I heard as my ears playing tricks on me.

We were shown to our Labor and Delivery room and started to settle in. Eventually, our nurse arrived and introduced herself. I could have sworn she said her name was Eliana but didn't hear her clearly. When she left the room to go get something, I asked Ross if he heard her name. He said he thought he heard her say Eliana but also didn't believe what he heard. When she came back in, we asked what her name was. It was exactly as we heard it and she proceeded to write it on the board. Not only was her name Eliana, but it was also spelled exactly the same as our baby girl.

Not wanting the looks on our faces to freak her out, I said to her, "You probably can tell from my file that we suffered a term stillbirth at 37 weeks and 5 days, and our daughter's name is Eliana, spelled the same way you spell yours."

She was shocked and said, "I just got goosebumps." I showed her the picture of Eliana with her name Eliana Elizabeth on the sign. The nurse said, "You aren't going to believe this, but my confirmation name is Elizabeth!" Double WHOA! She then explained to us that her usual shifts are at night and that this shift with us was an extra shift she just happened to pick up. This detail as we started Jeremiah's birth story was set off with such sentiment. Eliana, our baby girl, was with us, and God wanted to make sure we knew that. Such a positive start to the induction process.

I had to tell someone that would really appreciate what had happened, so I messaged Molly. Just as we were, Molly was also in awe of what happened. I mentioned to her that another friend while praying in Eucharistic Adoration received from the Holy Spirit that God is protecting us and Eliana is there and like the big sister, she was ready to usher Jeremiah into the world. This was a beautiful thought to which Molly added, "You have so much support around you, lots of light and you are highly protected." I shared that I was feeling very uplifted emotionally and this would explain a lot of that.

It took the induction hours to get started as there was so much paperwork to get done prior. We finally got started around 1:30 PM. To pass the time, Ross worked while I listened to my daily podcasts in between praise and worship music. I also had multiple chats with various family members and close friends. I got on and off the bed, spent some time on the ball, trying anything to get my contractions going but it was slow in coming.

I had been induced with Natalie and had started to get very strong contractions within an hour of being induced. Though I was induced with Natalie after my due date, I was still certain that this induction would have gone as fast, if not faster, as it was my 4th child. Even Eliana's induction moved fasted; however, I chalked it up to different medications being administered.

At around 6:15 PM, I asked Ross to pray the Rosary with me so we could hopefully get this show on the road. After praying the Rosary, I went back to my phone and noticed a new message from Geoffrey whom I had been speaking to over chat most of the day. He said, "This is going to sound strange, but there are so many divine beings with you. Mother Mary is there."

I said to him, "Ross and I were just praying the Rosary. It is said when you pray the Holy Rosary, the Blessed Mother of Jesus is there in Spirit." I told him I felt the strength of the presence of all those spirits around me and specifically, I felt a lot of peace which was unexplainable, given the circumstances.

Geoffrey then specifically said he saw in the room with us Eliana, Natalie, Grandpa Kirby, Natalie's Grandma and others he couldn't make out. He said it was just so bright in there, like full of daylight though it was already nighttime. He then said Natalie was the boss in the room, keeping everyone praying for us and maintaining calmness. He then said Eliana and another little boy are basically attached to me, but he didn't know who the boy was. I then said to him the little boy was Matthew, the baby I lost the summer before at 11 weeks. Matthew did not progress further than

6 weeks 5 days gestation and I eventually miscarried at 11 weeks. Because this loss was so early, the jury had been out for me. In my heart, I had an inclination he was a boy, so we named him Matthew. But Geoffrey was the first to ever confirm what I had known in my heart to be true.

At around 9:30 AM, the doctor came in to check again and I was between one to three cm dilated after seven hours. Not the news we wanted to hear. As they had maxed out the medication they started with, they offered me the option of a balloon to try to open my cervix more before administering other meds. At first, I tried the balloon without the epidural and though the pain was manageable, the discomfort was not conducive to sleep.

I proceeded to ask for the epidural as I really needed to get some sleep. One of the doctors tried to dissuade me from this as she indicated we likely had a long way to go and taking the epidural this early could have me lying down for a very long time and with no food. At around 1:30 AM, I got the epidural and went to sleep.

In the morning around 6:30 AM, the doctors came to remove the balloon and check me again. I was only five cm dilated and the baby was still high. Not ideal but they decided now was the time to start me on Pitocin.

By about 12 pm on October 8, one day after we checked in and started the induction, I was just seven cm dilated. It had been a full 24 hours at this point since the induction started. Jeremiah's birth had now surpassed both Natalie (13 hours) and Eliana (17 hours) in terms of time and was set to surpass Alexander's 27.5 hours of labor.

Ross and I were totally shocked. How was it possible that our 4th child was taking the longest to come out? We recalled many stories of people who barely made it to the hospital with their 2nd, 3rd, 4th, or 5th child. It is said, the more kids you have, the faster this is supposed to go because your body remembers what to do. It was clear at this point my body had amnesia! This was by far a lesson in patience and faith.

Finally, at 6 PM, I was fully dilated; however, the baby was still high up. At this point, Dr. O took the decision to break my water and give the baby fifteen minutes to see if he dropped down to where we needed.

During those fifteen minutes, I was overcome with emotion. This was it; he was almost out. It wouldn't be long now. I was transported back to this point in Eliana's birth. Pushing out a baby and when she arrived, there was deafening silence and the pain that came with that.

I was given the cue to push. After a few solid pushes, his head started to crown and I was told to pause pushing while the doctor doing the catching did a check. I then heard her say to Dr. O that we have a nuchal. Dr. O then asked her how tight. She then replied tight. From the look on Ross' face, I could tell he didn't understand what was being said. Most likely, like me, he was caught up in his own set of emotions and PTSD from Eliana's birth. They then said, "Ok, we want you to do only half pushes so we can easy the baby out." And I did just that. As Jeremiah's head and neck came out with the cord around his neck, I saw the look of concern on Ross' face as he was now clued in to what I knew from the doctors' conversation a few minutes before. A couple final pushes and he was out.

The minute he was out and in the doctor's arms, I broke down into tears. He was here as God promised. I looked up to Heaven and thanked God for His faithfulness and promises kept.

Simultaneously, I noticed there was no crying. They unwrapped the cord from around his neck and started to suction his nose and mouth and rub him vigorously. After what felt like forever, he started to cry. It wasn't a cry like Alexander or Natalie who screamed their lungs out, but it wasn't silence like Eliana. They placed him in my arms and I just cried and cried, overwhelmed with so much emotion. He was here; He was safe; Thanks be to God.

Chapter 25

The nurse took Jeremiah to get his weight, height and clean him off. It was required that we stay in the L&D room for a few hours while the epidural wore off. Once clean, they brought Jeremiah back to see if he would breastfeed. He was able to latch; however, I noticed he was making a weird grunting noise as he nursed. I drew this to Ross' attention as well as the nurse.

Now attuned to the weird noise he was making, I noticed he was also doing it while he wasn't nursing. It was not a noise we had experience with Alexander and Natalie so once the pediatrician arrived, we brought this to their attention.

The pediatrician indicated that sometimes when the delivery is fast i.e., the time between the water bag breaking and the baby coming out, some babies need additional time to transition to the outside world. The doctor and nurses assured us this was not unusual and that in most cases the baby's breathing regularizes within a few hours. During their check of his vitals, they suctioned his nose and mouth again to expel additional excess fluid and we agreed to wait a few hours.

While we waited for the anesthesia to wear off, our first call was to the kids to introduce them virtually to their brother. They were so happy and excited. It was important for us to call them and show them their brother, so they were assured he and I were all right, thus alleviating their worry. After our call with the kids, we continued to share pictures of Jeremiah with our family and friends who were anxiously awaiting his arrival over the past thirty hours of labor. Everyone was overjoyed and excited about the happy news.

Three hours after Jeremiah was born, I regained feeling in my legs and the nurses were ready to move us over to the postpartum wing. We were on to the next step of the journey and one step closer to going home. It was now almost 10:30 PM and we had had quite a long day. Upon arriving at the room, I noticed all the rainbows decorating our room door and Jeremiah's crib. I wasn't sure what to make of it until the nurses came in and handed us extra reading material which referred to our rainbow baby as well as acknowledging our loss of Eliana. This was such a beautiful and meaningful sentiment as we were having an immense moment of joy but also holding feelings of loss all at the same time.

Once settled into the room with Jeremiah back in our arms, Ross and I spoke about our individual concerns over his weird breathing. We were now three hours plus post birth, and it didn't seem to improve as they said it would. It was late and we were tired but neither of us wanted to sleep with Jeremiah continuing to make the strange breathing noise, so we called for the nurse. She said he was likely still transitioning and that this happens sometimes. We told her we understood it was likely transitioning, but we were not comfortable with how he was breathing and wanted to insist that the pediatrician from the NICU come back to reevaluate him.

Per our request, the pediatrician came back with a NICU nurse. They checked his vitals, which were good, and then tried to get a reading with the oxygen (O^2) monitor which was not working well. Due to this, she asked if she could take Jeremiah to the NICU to use the O^2 monitor there to ensure they got an accurate reading.

As we waited, Ross and I agreed that we were probably overreacting but given what happened to Eliana, we preferred to take this overly cautious step rather than have something happen to Jeremiah overnight while we slept.

About thirty minutes passed before the pediatrician returned. As she entered the room, we noticed she did not have Jeremiah with her and had a more serious look of concern on her face. She explained that Jeremiah's O^2 levels were around 86 which was a lot lower than they would have liked to see and so they were keeping him in the NICU to evaluate him for the next few hours and monitor him for signs of infection. It seemed as though he swallowed a decent amount of fluid on the way out. They also indicated that since I had gestational diabetes, they were going to monitor his glucose as well.

At around 1 AM, she returned to give us an update. She said after their evaluation, they decided to admit Jeremiah to the NICU as his O^2 levels remained in the high 80's and that at this point, he should be at minimum over 95. As a result, they were putting him on oxygen via a nose piece to see if they could help get his O^2 levels up. They also took the decision to start him on antibiotics to safeguard against infection related to swallowing the fluid. She explained that during the descent into the birth canal, babies are squeezed, and this squeezing helps to expel fluid from their lungs. In cases where the baby's descent is quick, they sometimes do not have enough of the fluid expelled and they need some extra help to dry out the excess fluid in their lungs.

All of this took Ross and me by surprise. We had thought we were just overacting, and they are now admitting him to the NICU. It was a lot to take in but we realized there was nothing we could do by trust in God and get some sleep.

At around 7 AM, the doctor returned to update us again saying that Jeremiah had shown signs of improvement with the O^2 he needed initially at 30 units but now down to 25 units. This was positive. She also indicated that they fed him 10 ml of formula at 2 AM and 10 ml at 5 AM as he was hungry. Though my plan was to exclusively breastfeed, my milk had not come in and he clearly needed to eat. She then said they change shifts at 8 AM and that another doctor would be taking over his case for the next 24 hours. We asked when we would be able to see him, and she said the doctor's usually do their patient evaluations in the morning so that any time after 10 AM would be good.

We thanked the doctor for her update and devised a plan to order breakfast, eat and shower before we headed to the NICU.

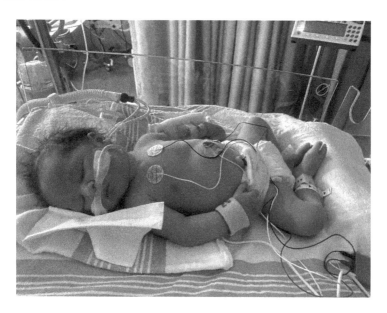

Upon entering the NICU, we followed the rigorous sani-
tizing regiment and then were shown to Jeremiah's cot. We
were taken back with all the cords and machines attached
to him and the large pieces of tap on his little face holding
the nose piece in place. Despite this, he looked comfortable
under the heater, sleeping peacefully; the grunting while
breathing had stopped.

While getting the update from the doctor, we asked
when they anticipated he would be released and able to
go home. The doctor said he thought he would be at a minimum in there for the next five days. We let that sink in. We
returned to our room in the postpartum unit since Jeremiah
was sleeping and it was very uncomfortable for me standing
and sitting in my state of recovering.

When we arrived in the room, Ross and I started to
second guess whether we did the right thing by insisting
on his reevaluation for grunting. We also now regretted
taking the stroller out of the car. Although the doctor had
said a minimum of five days, we were told things could turn
around quickly and he could be released earlier so we held
on to hope he would be released with me the next day.

We visited Jeremiah throughout the day and though
hesitant because of all the cords, I held him for skin-to-
skin contact with the help of the kind nurses. At this point,
the updates we got from the overnight nurse and the day-
time nurse were positive and upbeat. This, coupled with his
numbers on the machines looking good to our untrained
eyes, we were optimistic. Adding to this optimism was
that despite the cords, I was able to nurse him for his 2 PM
feeding. Everything seemed to be headed in the right direction, despite the results from his x-ray that morning confirming he did have fluid in his lungs.

It was a lot to take in, but we remained positive.

That day, I also had a visit from the lactation consultant at the hospital. She had visited to deliver me a breast pump with some reading material and tried to encourage me to pump for Jeremiah so when he was ready to eat more, I would have my supply in. I had nursed Alexander and Natalie for over two years each and I knew it was just a matter of time before my milk came in full force. I insisted it was not necessary for me to pump as my milk would come in. I also firmly voiced my concern that if I started to pump and my milk came in with no baby to nurse, it would be harder for me and that I just rather keep doing what I was doing by nursing him in the NICU and allowing it to come in naturally. She disagreed with my approach and made this known and we got a bit curt with each other. She meant well and I regretted how I was with her as she was just trying to help and let me know that even though he was in the NICU, he would still need my milk. After she left and I really reflected on why I had been so "not nice", I realized I had significant residual feelings from my milk coming in after Eliana dying and not having a baby to nurse. Though this situation with Jeremiah was different, it also felt terribly similar.

At around 5 PM, we returned to his bedside so I could attempt to nurse him again for his scheduled feeding. We were greeted by a new nurse on duty and I expressed my desire to nurse him again as he had nursed four times successfully earlier in the day. That visit with him, unfortunately, did not go as smoothly as the others. While trying to nurse Jeremiah, he refused to wake up to latch properly. I passed this off as regular baby business; however, the nurse disagreed and said I was causing his O^2 levels to drop. I explained to her that he had latched and successfully nursed on both sides earlier, but she eventually took him from me, woke him up and started to feed him formula with a bottle. This was very disheartening as I felt she could have helped me wake him up to nurse, versus filling him up on only formula. Also, the manner in which she told me I was the cause of his oxygen dropping came off harsh and all I was trying to do was feed him.

All of a sudden, while she was feeding him, he started to choke on the formula as the flow of the nipple was too fast for him due to his strong draw. Ross and I flashed each other a look where I knew we were equally annoyed at how this visit was going. She then changed the nipple and successfully completed his feeding.

After changing his diaper, he was returned to my arms to sleep for a while and all his vitals settled down. I needed him and he needed me and all day while we were together, his vitals got better. Ross could see how visibly upset the whole feeding situation got me and kept reassuring me that Jeremiah needed me and the numbers on the monitors clearly showing that.

As if the visit had not been bad enough, the nurse then gave us a dose of reality which we had not gotten before nor were prepared to hear. She said that if Jeremiah could not take a bottle or boob without being stressed out, they would have to put in a feeding tube through his nose and into his stomach so he could be fed easier and without stress. After a day of so many positive steps, feedings and positivity from the earlier nurses, we were not receptive to the idea of the feeding tube.

Emotionally and physically drained, we decided to retreat to our room for a bit before his next feeding. While in the room, Ross and I decided that I should just let the nurse feed him with the bottle at 8 PM as I was feeling quite dejected after the drama at the 5 PM feeding. We visited him for a short while after they fed him and then returned to our room. At about 9 PM, the doctor came to our room and expressed concern that Jeremiah wasn't where they thought he should be 24 hours after the start of their interventions. As a result, they recommended we put in a feeding tube which would go through his mouth directly into his stomach; this was to give his body a break from feeding and allow them to increase the airflow from 30 to 40 liters.

Four hours later at 2 AM, we were awakened by the NCIU doctor turning the lights on in our room and him requesting to speak with us. He indicated that instead of Jeremiah getting better with the latest intervention at 9 AM, he was getting worse. Because of this, he needed to have us sign some paperwork giving them permission to intubate him and administer surfactant if things continued to deteriorate. He said that he is now believing his initial diagnosis was not fully correct and that although Jeremiah was 37 weeks and 3 days and considered full term, he believed that my blood sugar management and gestational diabetes caused him to have immature lungs in addition to transitional tachypnoea of the newborn (TTN). We had literally been woken out of a deep sleep, so his explanations came fast with many words and terms we did not understand. OUCH! Did he just imply I didn't manage my blood sugar well enough, and I caused him to have immature lungs?

We signed what he wanted us to sign and then sat like two deer caught in the headlights with me feeling like I was a deer run over by the car. Not sure what he had said and wanting to ask him clarifying questions, I reached out to Georsan, my neonatologist bestie, for advice. She gave me a list of questions to ask and said to me over chat, "I know it feels like he's taking a step back, but he's just experiencing the extended version of TTN. Think of surfactant as lung lubricant. And he just used up his a little too quickly." As it had been many times before, Georsan's expertise provided comfort and reassurance.

When we got to the NICU, we asked if they could page the doctor so we could talk to him again. We then proceeded to Jeremiah's cot and was taken back at his appearance now on the CPAP face mask. It was hard to see him looking worse now than earlier with more cords, attachments and tape.

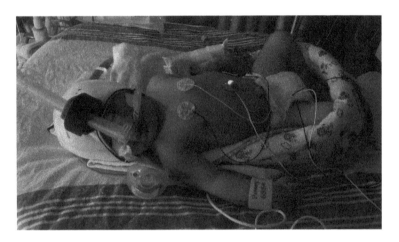

The doctor arrived and I started with question #1 that Georsan had sent me. "Will you leave him intubated and let him rest take it out immediately after the surfactant?" The doctor said he may leave it in for a few hours or a day, but it would all depend on how he takes to it. I then looked down at my phone and asked the next question regarding feeding by tube or IV. The doctor indicated they would use the IV and stop food temporarily. I then looked down at my phone again. However, the third question had a big technical word

I was not sure how to pronounce so I showed the doctor my phone so he could read the question himself.

Before he answered the question, he asked to whom I was talking.

I replied that we are consulting with my high school friend who is a neonatologist trained in Ireland and teaching neonatology in Bahrain. He then seemed relieved I was talking to another professional and answered the question. I explained to him that we did not want him to think we were second guessing him but just wanted to talk to our friend to help us understand what was happening as it was all new to us and, as he could imagine, very stressful. I also told him, which was true, that Georsan said she fully agreed with all the steps they had taken so far and that they were doing a good job. This seemed to put him at ease. It was almost four in the morning now and all our questions were answered, so we headed back to the room.

Not able to sleep, I recalled my words to my brother Michael earlier in the year when his daughter Everlynn spent almost a month in the NICU in Trinidad; "You need to ask people to pray for Everlynn's healing and for you and Cathrine to have strength." Though Jeremiah had been in the NICU for 36 hours already, I had not heeded my own advice given to Michael just months before. My reasoning at the time was that I was assured that though we were walking a rocky path with Jeremiah, God had promised this child to me and He was just making for a more inter-esting story and thus, my faith remained strong and without doubt. However, that morning, I was corrected by the Holy Spirit and was told that raising Jeremiah up in prayer for his healing doesn't mean I wavered in my faith that God will keep His promise, but that it was an essential part of the way in which God was going to keep His promise and what we needed to do.

> **Note to reader:** *The updates highlighted below and throughout the remaining chapters are the actual updates sent to our prayer warriors, family and close friends while Jeremiah was in the NICU.*

Update on Jeremiah: *Monday, October 10, 2022 – 4:46AM*

Call for Prayers

We noticed a few hours after birth, Jeremiah was not breathing in a way that made us comfortable so we asked the doctors to recheck him. Upon rechecking him, they agreed that he was, indeed, having breathing issues and he was admitted to the NICU Saturday night and he remains there currently. At first, it looked like due to his quick delivery (i.e. from water bag bursting to his birth), he swallowed some fluid and wasn't able to expel what was in his lungs which is usually squeezed out during birth.

The initial interventions taken by the NICU were to treat what they call transitional tachypnoea of the newborn (TTN).

They initially were treating him only for the TTN which is apparently very common. However, despite the interventions taken earlier, he hadn't been improving like they would have liked. So, they recommended at 9 PM on Sunday putting in a feeding tube and putting him on a high flow of oxygen using a face mask. We were seeing some improvement with this course of action; however, as of 2 AM Monday, the doctor did not think the improvement was sufficient and noted a regression of sorts which resulted in the reevaluation of his initial diagnosis to now include the complications of TTN coupled with immature lungs. Essentially, the doctor thinks it's possible that it is not only a case of swallowed fluid in his lungs but also his lung development was impacted by the gestational diabetes and are what they refer to as immature lungs despite his weight of 7lbs 9oz.

They are seeing this current course of action through with the higher O2 and what not and have seen some improvements. However, in order to go home, he needs to be able to sustain the right levels of O^2, breathing rate and heart rate to go home in various scenarios.

If this doesn't improve shortly, they will move to administering surfactant which is a medication to help his lungs. (Your body makes this on its own but sometimes with babies with immature lungs, this gets used up and not replaced quickly enough.) This course of action will require him to be intubated. It remains to be seen if this will be necessary, but it is the direction it can go quickly which is where we are at the moment.

That said please prayer for Jeremiah as well as Ross and I and the kids.

Chapter 26

After a few hours of sleep, the resident from Dr. O's practice came to check on my recovery and indicated they were ready to release me. Although she knew, I explained that Jeremiah was in the NICU, and I was not ready to go home. I asked if there was any way I could stay longer as we felt he was at a critical stage of his recovery, and we needed to be close by. She said she would discuss it with Dr. O and get back to us.

About an hour later, Dr. O came by and said he was working on trying to get us another night so we could be close to the baby. Within fifteen minutes of his visit, he updated us with a positive response. The nursing staff offered us an overflow room which was on the same floor; we just needed to change rooms. This room was only for one more night, but we were so grateful.

The hospital staff were so considerate of our situation that the nursing coordinator who approved the extra night stopped by to check in on us. She was a kind woman and fully empathized with our situation, having had a NICU baby herself. She explained that because of her experience of having a child in the NICU, she has always done what she could in her position to provide overflow rooms for parents like us when possible. We thanked her for her kindness and God for His mercy and grace.

Update on Jeremiah: Monday, October 10, 1:20PM

Thanks be to God for His blessings and mercies. He is faithful.

We saw Jeremiah 10:30 AM which was after we last saw him at 3:30 AM.

They as indicated at 2 AM they put him on CPAP which is essentially a baby mask that pushes pressurized air into the lungs. They initially started doing this with a high level of O_2 but as he responded favorably, reduced it with a goal of getting it to 21% which is the amount of oxygen regularly in a room.

We tried to visit at 6 AM but they were changing his IV so we couldn't go and didn't make it back there until 10:30 AM.

When we walked in at 10:30 AM, his whole set up changed. From the French Fry Tray with the CPAP mask to a full incubator with CPAP. We were a bit taken back by the set up; however, the monitor looked promising and he did look comfortable.

We were informed by the doctor and nursing staff that they do not at this point need to intubate him or do the surfactant because the CPAP has worked well and he has been able to fully wean off of the O_2 with the assistance of the CPAP. He has also been able to maintain 100% O_2 saturation, keep his breathing rate and other vitals within range.

Amen for good news and progress in the right direction.

Over the next few hours into the evening, they will attempt to remove the CPAP and see if he can keep his breathing, O_2 and vitals within an acceptable range. If he does they will move to trying him with food again. If he does not hold steady on his own he will go back on the CPAP and we will discuss the next course of action.

They will also do another X-ray this afternoon to reevaluate his lungs. Against what it was. In addition to retest cultures to rule out infection.

We will go visit him again once he is up.

I have officially been discharged but the hospital has been kind enough to offer us a boarding room until tomorrow to stay in as Jeremiah is still here.

Thank you for all your prayers and support. We definitely feel them and are uplifted as is Jeremiah.

> *Psalm 121: I will lift up mine eyes unto the hills, from whence cometh my help. My help cometh from the Lord, which made heaven and earth.*

Seeing Jeremiah in the incubator was beyond hard. When we walked in, we had naively assumed that when we saw him at 3 AM, it was the worst we would have seen as that in itself was a shocking sight. However, we were wrong. He was now in a full out incubator looking like a very sick baby. The nurse and doctor tried to reassure us that despite all the extra hardware, his numbers were good and he was doing well. It was hard to reconcile what we were seeing and what we were being told. On top of all that was going on, when we walked into the NICU, we recognized a familiar face. It was our neighbor Bri whom I had mentioned to Ross days before when we were in Labor and Delivery. I thought she was a Labor and Delivery (L&D) nurse in this hospital. On the walk in, we said "Hi" briefly but upon noticing the change in set up at Jeremiah's station our attention was quickly diverted.

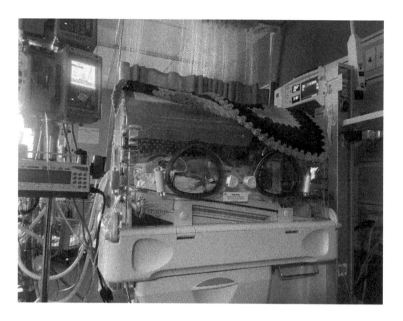

I could tell it was equally hard for Ross, as it was for me to see him like that. The feeling of helplessness sunk in, and we couldn't help but feel things were going in the wrong direction. Both of us becoming very emotional over the whole situation, we decided to head back to the room to regroup. As we walked out of the NICU to head back to our room, I heard Bri call out to us as she jogged up.

She said she was sorry after all we had been through with Eliana that Jeremiah was in the NICU, but she wanted to reassure us that although it looked bad in there, she had seen many babies with Jeremiah's condition turn around very quickly with the CPAP. She also said the doctor on his case was very good and thorough so although things may be progressing slowly, it's just her cautious approach. She said we could rest assured that when he was released, it was because she was 100% sure that he was ready to go home. This was exactly what we needed to hear.

What were the chances that the morning we walked out the NICU feeling shaken on the path set out in front of us that God would have our neighbor of four years, L&D nurse, to pick up an extra shift in the NICU and was the one who would be providing us words of comfort and reassurance? We didn't know the doctors and nurses in the NICU, but we knew Bri and she knew what we had been through with Eliana. So, when she said what she did, we took comfort in her experience and words. God sending us the much-needed assurances and support via Bri that morning was a miracle; perfect timing as usual and we were so grateful for His mercy.

Update on Jeremiah: *Monday, October 10, 10:10 PM*

Thank you for your continued prayers.

At the 5 PM consult with the doctor, I was informed that Jeremiah had fiddled with his CPAP and had been observed off of it briefly and was not maintaining his ranges for breathing and O^2 to their liking. This, coupled with the third X-ray showing improvement but still signs of immature lungs, they decided to put off his test run without the CPAP and just nose tubes.

Though not coming off the CPAP for his big test was disappointing, the doctor also indicated the surfactant no longer looked like an appropriate course of action for Jeremiah. This was due to the fact that he was able while on the CPAP to show all the right types of improvement and milestones that should he fail the "test" it would be recommended to put him back on CPAP and just let his lungs mature with time. According to the doctor this could be hours, days or weeks.

The X-ray plus his physical exam also moved us away from a possible pneumonia diagnosis.

They also indicated since his cultures came back clear, he was on his last dose of antibiotics.

Lastly, they indicated he was fussing due to empty stomach, so they decided to restart feeding via the feeding tube (combo of formula and BM).

Though this news was not all what we wanted to hear, it was still very much positive and further steps in the right direction.

I returned to the room and within an hour, I was called by the nurse to come hold Jeremiah as he was awake and active. I finished up getting more milk for him and headed back over.

When I got there, I noticed Jeremiah was swaddled which made him easier to hold. I also noticed his CPAP head gear was gone.

The nurse came over and explained Jeremiah decided that he was done with CPAP and pulled it off as well as other things so they monitored him and gave him a chance at just the nose tubes.

I held him for 45 minutes and from what I could see, he was managing within range. The nurses also said similar.

At 8 PM, he was fed again with more BM and formula, still via the feeding tube.

They will be monitoring him overnight with just the nose tubes and decide whether they could take out the feeding tubes and introduce food tomorrow via mouth.

You will keep him in perfect peace, Whose mind is stayed on You, Because he trusts in You (Isaiah 26:3)

We continued on the rollercoaster of emotions between the 5 PM consult and the 8 PM feeding. When I was called to come down to the NICU because he was up and ready to hold, I hustled to finish pumping and getting ready to go over to see him. Ross had gone home to see the kids and grab some extra clothes as we had been in the hospital a lot longer than anticipated when we packed. When I arrived at his bedside, I was again taken back but this time in a good way. Jeremiah was no longer in the incubator but back in a cot. He no longer had the CPAP on and he had a feeding tube down his nose instead of his mouth. The nurse explained that Jeremiah must have overheard the doctor say she was not removing the CPAP and decided on his own he was done with it and ripped it off his face along with all the cords on him. I laughed proudly and said, "Good for you, buddy!" She explained further that since the CPAP was off, they took the opportunity to observe him and made the decision he no longer needed it and they put him back on the nose piece. Bri was right; within hours, we had moved leaps and bounds. It was incredible to witness the power of prayer firsthand. I gave thanks to God for His goodness and for answering prayers.

Update on Jeremiah: Tuesday, October 11, 5:10 PM

Jeremiah continues to do well on the airflow nose piece. After posting good stats on the four units of pushed air since yesterday at 6:30 PM, they lowered it to two units at around 2:30 PM to see how he does. This is an important step as he needs to be fully off the airflow and post good stats in multiple situations for at least 24 hours before he gets discharged.

Going down to two units is a big step because if he does well they will remove the feeding tube and feed him by mouth. And then continue to study him.

They are also monitoring his blood sugar but have increased his food intake to ensure the sugar levels aren't due to not enough food.

They also are keeping an eye on a slight case of jaundice.

Ross and I have officially checked out the hospital but have 24-hour access to Jeremiah. We will go back tonight to talk to the doctor and get an update as well as drop off more food for him.

Thank you for your continued prayers and support.

> *"Therefore I tell you, whatever you ask for in prayer, believe that you have received it, and it will be yours –* (Mark 11:24).

The extra night provided by the hospital, Jeremiah's miraculous progress and the excellent care he was receiving put us in a place where we were ready to go home on Tuesday. I had not seen the big kids since the Friday before and really looked forward to reuniting with them. School pick up at 3 PM fell perfectly in between Jeremiah's 2 PM and 5 PM feeds, so we decided it was the perfect time to leave.

The day before, when Ross was going home to see the kids, he offered to take the stroller and car seat with him. We had at this point significantly discussed the empty car seat going home and after the emotional day we had, I did not want Ross to shoulder that burden alone, though I knew he would have preferred it that way to spare me the pain. So, I insisted he leave the stroller in the room and when we left, we would walk out together with the empty car seat together.

It was time. Time for us to walk out with the empty car seat. So much had changed in the last eighteen hours that our hearts were finally ready to take the walk as we were assured that we were coming back for him. It was just a matter of time.

After thanking all the staff for their kindness and accommodation, we began walking out to the car. As we passed the reception desk, the lady there noticed our stroller and said, "Congratulations!" I heard Ross quickly say, "Remember, I told you there is no baby in here; he's in the NICU." I assumed he must have told her this when he ran down to the car in order to avoid exactly what had just happened and any pain it would have caused me. He had witnessed firsthand my devastation, leaving the hospital without Eliana. I could tell he wasn't pleased it happened, but I just smiled at him and said, "It's ok I'm ok. It's different. We are coming back for him."

The kids were totally surprised to see me and assumed that the baby was also in the car. We had to explain to them that he was still in the hospital but would be coming home soon. After coming home without Eliana over a year before, they, too, needed to be reassured Jeremiah was coming home eventually; it was just a matter of time.

I went to the 5 PM feed alone to drop off the breastmilk and spend some time with him. Then Ross and I returned at 8 PM, dropped off more milk, had a quick visit and rushed home to shower and I pumped to drop off the 11 PM feeding.

At this point, I had managed to pump enough extra to cover his 2 AM, 5 AM and 8 AM feedings. It was a long day. We had gotten home after midnight. I had already started to feel the effects on my recovering postpartum body. due to going back and forth between home and the NICU. There was a lot of sitting in the car and in the NICU, which is never good postpartum. So, when we finally crawled into bed, I was so grateful for a good night's sleep.

The next morning, as planned, we took the kids to school and decided to get breakfast at a cute café in the area before we went. We had had hospital food for five days, so it was really nice to have some delicious and healthy food.

When we arrived at the NICU, we were once again totally surprised. Most of the cords were gone and I couldn't put my finger on it, but something else was different. He looked so good, like a peaceful healthy baby minus the feeding tube in his nose. The nurse then said, "We took out the airflow nose piece and he has been maintaining his levels on his own." Until she said this, I had not noticed he no longer had the airflow on his nose. Ross laughed at me saying it was the first thing he noticed when he walked in. What a wonderful surprise. The nurse then indicated that they wanted me to try to nurse him for the 11 AM feeding to see how he did, so we stayed there and we took turns holding him.

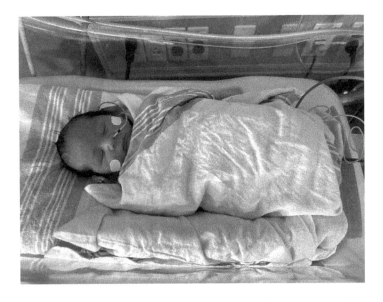

At this point, I was in a fair amount of pain sitting down. We tried the ring pillow, the boppy and several positions to try to alleviate the pain and discomfort but it didn't help much. The only option was to go back home but I refused, as it was very important for me to nurse him at 11 AM and see how he did.

Around 10:50 AM, he began to fuss as he was clearly hungry, so the nurse gave me the go ahead to nurse him. He latched like a pro and nursed like he had been eating via mouth since birth. He nursed for twenty minutes and maintained his O^2 saturation level and his other vitals were great. As soon as feeding time was done, we left as I was now in a tremendous amount of pain and needed to lie down. Despite my physical pain, we were overjoyed at the successful morning he had had. Though they were still monitoring his blood sugar and there was still some jaundice, things were looking up and we focused on that.

Update on Jeremiah: Wednesday, October 12, 11:45 AM

Thanks be to God!

Jeremiah is making great progress!

We arrived and were just totally surprised!

From midnight last night when we left him to this morning! The nose airflow is now gone and he was doing great on his saturation, breathing and vitals. Honestly I didn't even notice it was gone until the nurse said so!

His sugars are also up so they are going to let me nurse him at 11 AM to see how he does stats wise as well as sugars.

So many positive steps for Jeremiah. Thank you for your continued prayers and support

> But he said to me, "My grace is sufficient for you, for my power is made perfect in weakness." Therefore, I will boast all the more gladly about my weaknesses, so that Christ's power may rest on me (2 Corinthians 12:9).

I left breastmilk for the 2 PM feeding and decided to stay home to rest my body. We returned at 5 PM and 8 PM to nurse him again and drop off enough milk for his overnight and 8 AM feedings.

After another restful night's sleep which my recovering body needed, we dropped the kids at school, had breakfast again at the café and headed to the hospital to spend time with Jeremiah.

We arrived ready for another day of back and forth. When we saw Jeremiah, he looked great. We noticed he no longer had the feeding tube in, and they had removed all the tape from his face. His little cheeks were bruised from the tape, and I thought to myself, "It was a good thing I rescheduled his newborn shoot because it would have been rough with those raw cheeks."

As we cuddled our little guy, the doctor came by to give us the morning update. She asked, "Are you ready to take him home because he's ready to go home?" If my heart could have jumped out of my chest in that moment, it would have! We excitedly said, "Yes, of course we are ready to take him home." The doctor said ok and started the discharge process.

We couldn't believe it! He was going home. As the time came closer to the conclusion of the discharge tests and requirements, Ross and I realized we had really not expected this, so we had nothing but the car seat. No baby bag, no blanket, no change of clothes. The NICU didn't require much in terms of clothes as he was swaddled most of the time. Under the swaddle, he had on a wrapped baby shirt and a diaper. We discussed the practicality of this outfit on this fall day in South Jersey. Realizing this, we asked the nurses if they had a sleeper or anything we could use to take him home. The nurse went into the donation basket in the back and found one newborn sleeper and gave it to us. She explained all the other sleepers were preemie which wouldn't fit as he wasn't a preemie; he was just a term baby that needed some help. Grateful for the one sleeper, we dressed him in the worn-out sleeper.

After several hours of waiting, he was discharged. They took his graduation photo from the wall and gave him his certificate. We graciously thanked the doctor and nurses and put him in the car seat. The car seat was no longer empty and we were walking out with our baby; the son

God told me I was having; the son I was promised. The update to our family and friends that day was the perfect picture of Jeremiah in his car seat saying, "destination home" along with the Bible verse, Lamentations 3:22-23: "The steadfast love of the LORD never ceases; his mercies never come to an end; they are new every morning; great is your faithfulness."

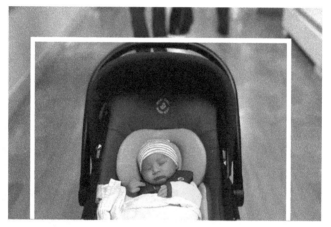

Destination Home

The steadfast love of the LORD never ceases; his mercies never come to an end; they are new every morning; great is your faithfulness

Lamentations 3:22-23

Chapter 27

W e arrived home to a fully decorated living room. It was apparent that over the weekend, the kids decorated the house with balloons, streamers and signs in anticipation of Jeremiah's homecoming. I could tell they had done it over the weekend as it was now Thursday, and the balloons were a bit deflated. Nevertheless, it was perfect. My mom had arrived a couple days before and had been anxiously awaiting his birth and subsequent release from the NICU. I felt for her and my dad as the past eighteen months had been hard on them. First, they lost a grandchild and then had two subsequent grandchildren spend time in the NICU.

Ross went to pick up the kids from school and decided to tell them while in the car that their brother had come home. As they entered the house, I could hear Alexander say, "Where is he? Where is he? I'm ready to see him!" in the sweetest whispered voice. They approached the pack and play where Jeremiah was swaddled and peacefully asleep and I could hear them gasp in wonder. Alexander then said, "Awww... Oh my goodness, he's adorable!" Natalie just gig- gled and started to smile, "He's a little munchkin. He has my nose, Mama."

We then asked them both to shower quickly so they would be able to hold him when he woke up. Alexander was the first to finish showering and come downstairs. He was anxious to hold him, so I told him to sit in the big armchair and I placed a nursing pillow on his lap to support his arms. As I placed Jeremiah in his arms, I could see the tears in his eyes. The brother he prayed for, the brother he always wanted was real and he was home safely. I felt overwhelmed with the relief and emotion coming from Alexander. Natalie then came downstairs and walked straight up to Alexander and Jeremiah and couldn't stop smiling. She was glowing with happiness. Soon after, it was her turn to hold Jeremiah. She was the proudest big sister and a natural at holding him.

My heart was full as I watched Alexander and Natalie. They had been through so much losing Eliana and now they were having a redeeming moment welcoming and holding Jeremiah for the first time. Jeremiah in no way replaced Eliana, but Alexander was right all those months ago when he said the things they missed out on with Eliana, they would be able to experience now with their brother. Our family was complete, and our broken hearts were full of love and gratitude.

 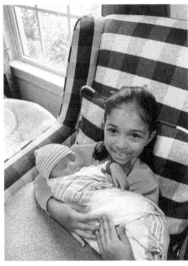

Alexander and Natalie meet Jeremiah for the first time.

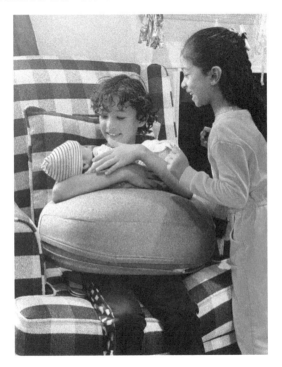

Chapter 28

A s we approached Eliana's second birthday, I reflected on all we had been through. What a journey! Often my mind is blown thinking of it all: the unimaginable lows; the miraculous highs and the numerous challenges overcome in between, all woven together with the thread of an ever-evolving faith and purpose covered in prayer and the love of God.

Every time I looked at Jeremiah since the day he was born it continues to be surreal. He has been an absolute blessing to our family and was the missing piece needed to put our broken hearts back together. His life as our rainbow baby has made us whole again in a way only God knew we needed. We will never be who we were before Eliana as she has forever changed us but Jeremiah, in his own way has also changed us. Without Eliana there would be no Jeremiah; and life without either of their existences is at this point unfathomable. So here we are.

God continues to be present in every moment of every day of my life and my relationship with Him is what fills me. If you have truly experienced the awesome and all-consuming love of God, you would know that the darkness which comes with the death of a loved one is overcome with the light and love of God.

We, here on earth have not been promised by God an easy life because we are each born with a purpose to learn or help others learn so we can evolve into who we are meant to be for His Glory. Free will, however, gave us a choice. We can accept God's purpose, or we can say no thank you and go our own way. In the end, the choice is ours. The only thing we have been promised is that He will always be with us and in my case, I held Him to that promise, and He delivered beyond my expectations. This book is my testimony to God's promise.

God is always there and ready for a relationship with us, no matter what we have done to offend Him, how much we have ignored Him or in some cases, the fact we didn't believe in Him at all.

But like in all aspects of life, the measure and strength of any relationship is always equal to what both parties put into it. It is through our relationship with the Lord that all other relationships in our lives can thrive and flourish, even our relationship with ourselves.

The peace that I feel in my spirit and the joy that fills my heart, despite all we have gone through, is fully attributed to the presence of the Lord in my life.

Thank you, sweet Savior, for your presence in my life and for our beautiful relationship. My life is yours, for your purpose and to glorify your Holy Name.

Give thanks to the LORD, call on his name; make known among the nations what he has done. Sing to him, sing praise to him; tell of all his wonderful acts. Glory in his holy name; let the hearts of those who seek the LORD rejoice (Psalm 105).

Photo Credit Kristen Nicotra of KArtocin Photography

Photo Credit Kristen Nicotra of KArtocin Photography

Photo Credit Kristen Nicotra of KArtocin Photography

Jeremiah's 1st Christmas (2022)

Jeremiah's 1st taste of food 5 months old,

Alexander, Natalie and Jeremiah celebrating Ross' Birthday 2023

Ross and Jeremiah 6-month-old in Breckenridge Colorado

On Wednesday March 2, 2022 while in Eucharistic Adoration praying the above vision was imparted to me by the Holy Spirit. I had never seen Eliana in her heavenly state before, so this was a beautiful and unexpected gift from the God. A glimpse at my eternity.

Artist Amy Bunnell Jones of @ajspalette on Etsy

Artist Create My Picture on Etsy

CPSIA information can be obtained
at www.ICGtesting.com
Printed in the USA
BVHW011913180523
664437BV00016B/216

9 781662 876172